Frank Gardner Noyes

An Account of the Soldiers' and Sailors' Monument

Frank Gardner Noyes

An Account of the Soldiers' and Sailors' Monument

ISBN/EAN: 9783337308469

Printed in Europe, USA, Canada, Australia, Japan

Cover: Foto ©ninafisch / pixelio.de

More available books at **www.hansebooks.com**

AN ACCOUNT

OF THE

SOLDIERS' AND SAILORS'

MONUMENT

ERECTED BY THE PEOPLE OF THE CITY OF

NASHUA, N. H.

IN THE YEAR EIGHTEEN HUNDRED EIGHTY-NINE,
IN HONOR OF THE MEN OF NASHUA
WHO SERVED THEIR COUNTRY DURING THE WAR OF
THE REBELLION, A. D. 1861-65.

Published by order of the City Councils. November, 1889.

NASHUA, N. H.
JAMES H. BARKER, CITY PRINTER.
1889.

RESOLUTION.

Providing for a memorial volume of the Soldiers' and Sailors' Monument and appropriation not exceeding two hundred and fifty dollars.

CITY OF NASHUA,

In the year of our Lord, one thousand, eight hundred and eighty-nine.

Resolved, By the Mayor and Aldermen and Common Council of the City of Nashua, in City Councils assembled as follows :—

That the Committee appointed to carry out the provisions of resolution number (978) nine hundred and seventy-eight, passed by the City Councils January 29th, 1889, be and is hereby authorized and requested to cause to be prepared and published a memoriol volume, which shall contain an historical account of the Soldiers' and Sailors' Monument erected as provided in said Resolution, together with the proceedings at the laying of the Corner-Stone, and at the Dedication of said Monument, including such papers and documents as said Committee may deem appropriate.

Said volume shall be prepared in such manner and form as said Committee may consider suitable, and the edition published shall consist of five hundred copies.

*　　*　　*　　*　　*　　*　　*

In Board of Aldermen, passed October, 22, 1889.

CHARLES H. BURKE, Mayor.
CHARLES S. BUSSELL, City Clerk.

In Board of Common Council, passed November 12, 1889.

HENRY P. WHITNEY, President,
GEORGE E. DANFORTH, Clerk.

LIST OF ILLUSTRATIONS.

THE MONUMENT, - - - - *Frontispiece.*
THE SOLDIER, - - - - *Opposite Page 17.*
THE SAILOR, - - - - *Opposite Page 67.*

CONTENTS.

	Page.
GITY GOVERNMENT,	9
RESOLUTION,	13
THE MONUMENT,	17
THE BUILDING COMMITTEE,	19
FIRST REPORT OF THE BUILDING COMMITTEE,	21
LAYING THE CORNER-STONE,	25
The Procession,	29
Announcement by His Honor, Charles H. Burke, Mayor of Nashua,	31
Address in honor of the Unknown Dead, by Comrade Frank G. Noyes, G. A. R.,	32
Address of Mayor Burke,	35
Masonic Ceremonies,	37
Address of the Grand Master,	38
List of articles deposited in Corner-Stone,	39
Oration by Colonel Frank G. Noyes,	45
SECOND REPORT OF THE BUILDING COMMITTEE,	53
ARRANGEMENTS FOR THE DEDICATION,	57
DESCRIPTION OF THE MONUMENT,	67
THE DAY,	75
THE PROCESSION,	81
THE DEDICATION,	93
Order of Exercises	96
Unveiling of the Monument and its delivery to the City by the Building Committee,	97
Acceptance in behalf of the City and address by Mayor Burke,	98
Dedicatory Ceremonies by the Grand Army of the Republic,	101
Oration by Charles H. Burns,	107
Closing Exercises,	119
FINAL PROCEEDINGS,	121

CITY GOVERNMENT.

CITY OF NASHUA, N. H.

CITY GOVERNMENT FOR THE YEAR 1889.

BOARD OF MAYOR AND ALDERMEN.

Hon. Charles H. Burke, (Mayor,) Chairman.

Charles S. Bussell, (City Clerk,) Clerk.

Ward 1. Charles T. Lund.
" 2. Edward T. Morrill.
" 3. Eugene D. Perrault.
" 4. William H. Beasom.
" 5. John D. Sullivan.
" 6. James C. Moody.
     Alphonse Burque.
     John J. Sullivan.
" 7. Ira H. Proctor.
" 8. George L. Bugbee.

CITY GOVERNMENT. (Continued.)

BOARD OF COMMON COUNCIL.

Henry P. Whitney, President.
George E. Danforth, Clerk.

Ward 1. Harry W. Ramsdell,
Edward M. Gilman.
" 2. Alfred W. Heald,
Charles E. Faxon.
" 3. John Ledoux,
Frank B. Stark.
" 4. Josiah N. Woodward,
James H. Barker.
" 5. Charles F. Sanders,
James Mulvanity.
" 6. Henry P. Whitney,
George F. Trowbridge,
Clarence A. Slate,
Frank P. Rideout,
Edmond D. Lucier,
James H. Moran.
" 7. George E. Holt,
Joseph L. Clough.
" 8. Harlan P. Wardwell,
William C. Leahy.

THE RESOLUTION.

RESOLUTION.

For the erection of a Soldier's Monument and appropriation not exceeding twelve thousand dollars.

CITY OF NASHUA,

In the year of our Lord, one thousand, eight hundred and eighty-nine.

Resolved, By the Mayor and Aldermen and Common Council of the City of Nashua, in City Councils assembled as follows :—

That a sum not to exceed twelve thousand dollars be and hereby is appropriated for a Soldiers' Monument, the said monument to be located on Abbot Square.

That the Mayor, two Aldermen, three Councilmen and three ex-soldiers of the War of the Rebellion be appointed a Committee to carry said resolution into effect. The same to be appointed by the Mayor in Joint Convention. The Mayor to be chairman of said Committee.

That the City Treasurer is authorized and instructed to issue two City notes for six thousand dollars. ($6000) each.

One payable in the year 1894. The second in 1895. The money to be used to meet the above appropriation.

In Board of Common Council, passed January 29, 1889.

     HENRY P. WHITNEY, President.
     GEORGE E. DANFORTH, Clerk.

In Board of Aldermen, passed January 29, 1889.

     CHARLES H. BURKE, Mayor.
     CHARLES S. BUSSELL, City Clerk.

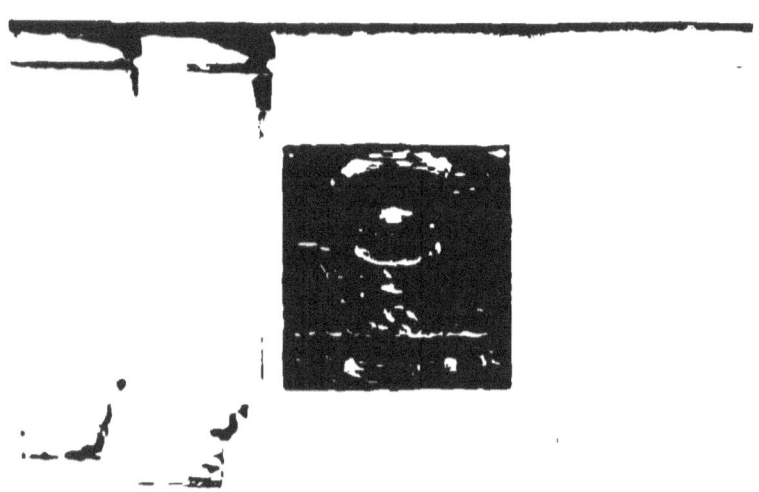

THE MONUMENT.

THE MONUMENT.

In pursuance of the provisions of the foregoing Resolution, a committee was appointed on the 29th day of January, 1889, called the BUILDING COMMITTEE OF THE SOLDIERS' AND SAILORS' MONUMENT, and was constituted and organized as follows:—

  CHARLES H. BURKE, Mayor, (Chairman.)

ALDERMEN, JOHN D. SULLIVAN, CHARLES T. LUND. COUNCILMEN. ALFRED W. HEALD, HARLAN P. WARDWELL, JAMES H. MORAN,	On part of the City Government.
CHARLES W. STEVENS, FRANK G. NOYES, ROYAL B. PRESCOTT, Secretary.	On part of the Veteran Soldiers.

The Building Committee immediately began its work. On the 4th day of February, circulars were issued, and advertisements were forthwith inserted in the leading architectural magazines and periodicals published in Boston, New York and Chicago, inviting designs, plans and proposals from architects, designers, builders and contractors. In response to these invitations, thirty-six drawing of plans and designs for a monument were submitted to the Committee within the time designated, namely, the 15th day of March, 1889. On that day the drawings were examined by the Committee in the room of the Mayor and Aldermen, and each exhibitor was given an opportunity, as advertised, to appear before the Committee and describe, explain and point out the merits of his design, and also state the estimated cost, or to offer direct bids or proposals for building the monument according to the plan or design submitted. Every design submitted was carefully examined by the full Committee. Most of the designs were presented by their respective authors, and ample time was given to each to fully acquaint the Committee with its merits, and actual or estimated cost.

The Committee after a patient and exhaustive examination of each plan, both separately and by comparison, selected and without a dissenting voice, voted to adopt the plan designed by Mr. T. M. Perry, architect for Messrs. Frederick & Field, quarrymen and builders, of Quincy, Mass., by whom the design was owned and submitted. The owners of the chosen design refused to sell, and declined to furnish it with plans and specifications, for other parties to estimate and bid upon. They offered to execute a contract to furnish all material and build a monument from the design, according to plans and specifications submitted, for a sum of money within the limit of the appropriation.

On the 31st day of March, a contract was executed by the Building Committee, in behalf of the City of Nashua, and Messrs. Frederick & Field, which provided for the erection of a monument on Abbot Square, which should be finished and ready for dedication on or before the 15th day of October, 1889.

REPORT OF THE BUILDING COMMITTEE.

REPORT OF THE BUILDING COMMITTEE.

NASHUA, N. H., MAY 7, 1889.

TO THE CITY COUNCILS :—

GENTLEMEN :—Your Committee appointed under the provisions of a joint resolution entitled :—"A Resolution for the erection of a Soldiers' Monument, and appropriation not exceeding twelve thousand dollars," passed January 29th, 1889, beg leave respectfully to report progress and state,

First :—That your said Committee in behalf of the City has executed a contract with Messrs. Frederick & Field, quarrymen and builders of Quincy, Mass., for the erection and completion of a suitable Monument to carry said Resolution into effect, on or before the 15th day of October next.

Second :—That your said Committee has made arrangements to lay the Corner-Stone of said Monument with appropriate ceremonies on Thursday afternoon, May 30th instant, Decoration Day.

Third :—That your said Committee begs respectfully to suggest that your honorable bodies take such action as you may deem proper, to be present officially on the occasion of laying the Corner-Stone on Abbot Square, at the time stated above.

Respectfully submitted,

In behalf of the Building Committee,

CHARLES H. BURKE, Mayor and Chairman.

Report read and accepted May 14, 1889, In Board of Aldermen,

CHARLES S. BUSSELL, City Clerk.

Accepted by the Common Council, May 28th, 1889.

GEORGE E. DANFORTH, Clerk.

LAYING THE CORNER-STONE.

LAYING THE CORNER-STONE.

On Thursday, May 30, the Corner-Stone was laid with imposing ceremonies by the Grand Master of Masons of New Hampshire, assisted by the proper officers of the Grand Lodge. The day being Decoration, or Memorial Day, was observed more generally than ever before in Nashua. The weather was all that could be desired, the atmosphere cool and bracing, the streets free from dust, and the sun shining out in all the delightfulness of a beautiful June day. Everything was apparently in harmony with the occasion, which was one that interested every citizen of Nashua, as well as the people of the surrounding towns, who came by thousands to witness the procession, listen to the orations, and in some manner express their interest in paying their respects to the veterans who stood between them and the wall of fire which raged so fiercely in the days of the Rebellion. The mills were closed and business was generally suspended, and this Memorial Day in Nashua will be remembered by those who participated, as one of the most historic in their lives. In the forenoon delegations from John G. Foster Post, No. 7, G. A. R., visited the older and outlying cemeteries, viz., the Nashua Cemetery, the Amherst Street Cemetery, the Hudson Cemetery, and the Harbor burying grounds, and decorated the graves of the heroic dead who served their country during the war of the Rebellion.

At 1.30 p. m., the comrades of the Grand Army of the Republic formed in line and marched to decorate the graves of veterans reposing in the Hollis Street Cemetery. The Grand Army column was formed on Main Street, right resting on Franklin Street, in the following order:—

>City Marshal, W. C. Tolles, with Platoon of Police.
>Chief Marshal, E. T. Perkins.
>Chief of Staff, E. D. Franklin.
>Chaplain, Rev. W. H. Moreland.
>Aids:—R. C. Duffy, C. H. Harris, Macy T. Shattuck, Charles Marden, L. F. Thurber, H. H. Putnam, John H. Fields, John D. Sullivan, George F. Perham, Ira S. Brigham, A. D. Walker, E. D. Eaton, Fred Runnells, William Kennedy and Joseph Ackerman.
>Second Regiment Band.
>Co. I. (Foster Rifles.) Second Regiment, N. H. N. G.
>Co. C., Second Regiment, N. H. N. G.
>Co. A, High School Cadets.
>Sons of Veterans as escort to John G. Foster Post, No. 7, G. A. R.
>John G. Foster Post, No. 7, G. A. R.
>Knights of Pythias.
>Orator and President of the Day.
>His Honor the Mayor.
>City Government.
>Invited Guests and Citizens in Carriages.

The column moved through Main and Kinsley Streets to the Cemetery, where the ceremony of decorating the soldiers' graves was performed by John G. Foster Post, No. 7, G. A. R., assisted by the Sons of Veterans. The column then returned through Hollis, Chestnut, Pearl and Main Streets to the City Hall, where a halt was made, and the battalion was formally turned over to Chief Marshal of the day, M. A. Taylor.

Here the line of procession for

LAYING THE CORNER-STONE

was formed, right resting on City Hall building, and marched to Abbot Square, through Main and Concord Streets, in the following order:—

THE PROCESSION.

City Marshal Tolles with Platoon of Police.
Chief Marshal, M. A. Taylor.
Chief of Staff, Eugene P. Whitney.
Aids:—Alvin S. Eaton, Charles S. Collins, H. A. Bowers, Patrick Lonergan, Frank H. Kellogg, Henry P. Whitney, W. D. Dodge and A. A. Hall.
Second Regiment Band, W. A. Cummings, leader,
Sam. N. Hoyt, drum major.

FIRST DIVISION.

Major J. E. Tolles, commanding battalion, and staff; Adjutant C. E. Faxon, Quartermaster George P. Kimball, Paymaster Charles A. Roby, and Chaplain George W. Grover.
Co. I, Second Regiment. N. H. N. G., Capt. E. H. Parmenter.
Co. C, Second Regiment, N. H. N. G., Capt. H. S. Stevens.
Co. A, High School Cadets, Capt. A. G. Shattuck.

SECOND DIVISION.

E. T. Perkins, Marshal, and Staff.
John G. Foster Post 7, G. A. R., Alfred Chase, Commander, Charles McGregor, Adjutant.
J. Q. A. Warren Camp, Sons of Veterans, Capt. George E. Cross.
Nashua Fire Department, Charles H. Whitney, Chief Engineer; Charles N. Colburn, George W. Piplar, George F. Adams, Frank B. Hale, Assistant Engineers.
Torrent Steam Fire Engine Company, S. R. Collins, Assistant Foreman.
Niagara Steam Fire Engine Company. L. I. Minard, Foreman.
Pennichuck Hose Company, J. F. Brown, Foreman.
Union Hook and Ladder Company, W. F. Barnes, Foreman.

THIRD DIVISION.

George E. Bagley, Marshal, and Staff.
Moody Drum Corps.
Canton A, Patriarchs Militant, Charles T. Lund, Commanding.
S. S. Davis Division, Knights of Pythias; First Lieutenant, David M. Rollins, Commanding.
Foster Rifles Drum Corps.
T. B. Crowley Conclave, Knight of Sherwood Forest, Arthur Sargent, Commanding.

THE PROCESSION.

FOURTH DIVISION.

L. P. A. Lavoie, Marshal, and Staff.
St. Jean Band, Anaclet Larivee, leader.
Division No. 1, A. O. H., Thomas McCarthy, President.
Division No. 2, A. O. H.. J. J. Doyle, President; William Molloy, Marshal.
Union St. Jean Baptiste Society, E. D. Perrault, President; P. D. Carden, Marshal.

FIFTH DIVISION.

George E. Heath, Marshal, and Staff.
Chelmsford Band.
St. George Commandery, K. T., Joseph Shattuck, Eminent Commander; George B. Bowler, Generalissimo; James H. Hunt, Captain General.
Trinity Commandery, K. T., Manchester; Charles C. Hayes, Eminent Commander; George I. McAllister, Generalissimo; Harvey L. Currier, Captain General.
Mt. Horeb Commandery, K. T., Concord; Frank L. Sanders, Eminent Commander; Charles F. Batchelder, Generalissimo; George O. Dickerman, Captain General.
Grand Commandery, Knights Templar, of New Hampshire.
Grand Lodge, A. F. and A. M., of New Hampshire in carriages: M. W. Grand Master, George W. Currier, Nashua; R. W. Deputy Grand Master, Frank D. Woodbury, Concord; R. W. Senior Grand Warden, John Pinder, Portsmouth; R. W. Junior Grand Warden, Charles C. Hayes, Manchester; R. W. Grand Treasurer, Joseph Kidder, Manchester; R. W. Grand Secretary, George P. Cleaves, Concord; Rev. Henry B. Smith, R. W. Chaplain, Nashua; George E. Beacham, W. Senior Grand Deacon, Great Falls; Henry A. Marsh, W. Junior Grand Deacon, Nashua; George C. Perkins of Lebanon, John K. Wilson of Manchester, Charles C. Danforth of Concord, Alfred R. Evans of Gorham, W. Grand Stewards; Joseph W. Hildreth, W. Grand Marshal, Manchester; John P. Bartlett, W. Grand Sword Bearer, Manchester; Nathaniel S. Gale of Penacook, John C. Bickford of Manchester, W. Grand Pursuivants; Samuel W. Emerson, Grand Tyler, Concord.
Orator, Colonel Frank G. Noyes; Mayor, Hon. Charles H. Burke, and Building Committee of the Soldiers' and Sailors' Monument.
City Government, ex-Mayors and Invited Guests, in carriages.

On the arrival of the procession at Abbot Square, the various bodies were skillfully massed about the foundation of the monument, while the thousands of spectators filled the streets and sidewalks bordering on the square.

The Mayor and members of the City Government, the Grand Master of Masons and his staff, the Orator of the Day, the President, the Orator and other officers of the day and evening of the Grand Army Post, together with the invited guests were escorted to seats on the grand stand and raised platform which had been temporarily erected south and west of the foundation.

LAYING THE CORNER-STONE OF THE SOLDIERS' AND SAILORS' MONUMENT.

The solemn ceremonies attending the laying of the Corner-Stone were then proceeded with in the following order :—

1. Announcement by His Honor, Charles H. Burke, Mayor of Nashua, as follows :—

Fellow Citizens :—

One of the beautiful usages of the Grand Army of the Republic on Decoration day, is to scatter flowers under a memorial arch, and listen to an address in honor of the Unknown Dead. This being Decoration day, the comrades of that order have been invited to perform those ceremonies around these foundation stones, before the Corner-Stone is laid. I therefore take pleasure in introducing to you the President of the day for the Grand Army of the Republic, Captain E. M. Shaw, who will take charge of that ceremony.

2. Strewing the foundation of the monument with flowers in honor of the Unknown Dead.

Captain Shaw then announced that John G. Foster Post, No. 7, would strew the foundation of the monument with flowers in accordance with the beautiful custom of the Order, and gave the necessary commands. The line of Veterans then marched slowly around, to the music of a dirge, and cast their floral offerings upon the foundation, as they passed by.

3. Address in honor of the Unknown Dead, (upon invitation of John G. Foster Post, No. 7, G. A. R.) by Comrade Frank G. Noyes.

The President of the day presented Comrade Noyes, who delivered the following address:—

ADDRESS.

Mr. Commander and Veterans:—

We have strewn the graves of our honored dead with the sweet flowers of spring. We have decorated them with the garlands of love. Let us now entwine chaplets from the flowers of memory and hope, and cast them forth with faith that favoring winds will waft them to decorate the last earthly resting places where thousands of our heroes repose in unknown graves.

While we cannot plant flags at the heads of all those graves, as you have placed them here to-day, we have the grateful satisfaction of knowing that what they fought for, now floats over them wherever they lie under the sod on the face of this broad country. The same old flag, that fired upon in 1861, brought us here to-day. The same old flag, that was unfurled from every hilltop, in every valley, and in every city, town and village throughout our loyal North; " and tearful eyes looked up to it, and firm knit hearts and planted feet were underneath, and dearer than life or home and sacred next to our faith and our God, is that old flag yet." We have assembled here, comrades, solemnly and devoutly to perform a sacred ceremony. We have come, to strew these sweet symbols of promise upon this foundation of the Soldiers' and Sailors' Monument, in honor of the memory of Unknown Dead. But we are here also to perform another duty. We have come to drop a tear to the memory of our fellow-soldiers who sleep their last sleep in unknown graves. We have come to mingle our tears of sympathy for those desolate homes whose remaining members have not even the sad consolation of scattering flowers over the graves of their loved and lost. And while we perform these sad, yet grateful duties, may we not indulge a generous impulse and extend our sympathies? May we not, at this sacred hour, throw the mantle of charity and forgiveness over the errors of our brothers, and let the Boys in Blue shed a sympathetic tear for the beareaved and desolate households of the Boys in Gray. The Boys in Gray were human,—they erred; Let the Boys in Blue assume a divine attribute and, to-day, forgive. Then it may be said :—

> "Sadly, but not up-braiding,
>   The generous deed was done,
> In the storm of the years that are fading,
>   No braver battle was won.
> Under the sod and the dew,
>   Waiting the judgment day,
> Under the blossoms the Blue;
>   Under the garlands, the Gray."

> "No more shall the war cry sever,
>   Or the winding river be red,
> They banish our anger forever,
>   When they laurel the graves of our dead.
> Under the sod and the dew,
>   Waiting the judgment day,
> Love and tears for the Blue.
>   Tears and love for the Gray."

Many of us have already forgiven. If there are any of you, my comrades, who have not, let me entreat you by the right of one who served for four long years under your flag, and whose proudest boast it is that no drop of disloyal blood ever flowed through his veins; let me entreat you by the precious blood shed; by the woe and desolation of mournful homes; aye, by the example of Him who watches alike over friend and foe, and who in the crisis of His persecution and in the bitterness of His woe, cried, "Father, forgive them, for they know not what they do." I entreat you to let the recording angel of heaven's chancery as he writes down this day's memorial, enter against names of us all that we have forgiven our enemies.

We have spoken of the unknown dead. UNKNOWN? They should not be unknown. When they lost their names with their lives, the pouring of that precious blood should have been a re-baptism, and the names of them at the re-christening should have been the same, and I would have it inscribed on the slab at the head of every grave now marked "Unknown", so that when the sad-eyed mourner should see the inscription on *any* grave she might say, "Here reposes my dead. At his re-baptism with his own heart's blood, he was named LOYALTY and here is his grave."

The Unknown Dead.

> "On Fame's eternal camping ground
> Their silent tents are spread,
> And glory guards with solemn round
> The bivouac of the dead."

Oh! dear unknown. To-day the same beautiful sunlight that floods the graves of our known dead; the same gentle wind that fans the blossoms we have placed upon these heroes' graves, lingers over the spot where rests the body of him for whom some aching heart is striving to still the longing, because the sad consolation of bearing a tribute of flowers to her dolized dead is denied her. To the memory of that vast army of the unknown—yet alas! only too well known and remembered—the chords of some heart are vibrating with a sad, unutterable longing, that to those here present who have with us the graves of our loved ones, can never be felt in all its pathos of wistfulness and hopelessness. THE UNKNOWN DEAD! There are none! Every hero who yielded his soul on the field of honor, and went to an unmarked and unrecognized grave, left behind him some faithful and devoted one, whose grief is the deeper, and whose tears fall the more bitterly, because her cry for the sad consolation of shedding them by her soldier's grave is a hopeless one. Ah! dear unknown, wherever you are this day sleeping! Though the only tribute upon your graves be the blossoms nature reverently places there; though the birds chant your only requiem; may the incense from these our offerings, gemmed by our tears, hallowed by the prayers sent forth from hearts full of sacred memories, reach you in your lonely, unvisited graves, and make your sleep sweeter in that dreamless peace which comes alike to the known and unknown who have joined the silent majority.

4 Address by His Honor, the Mayor, as follows :—

Fellow Citizens:—

More than twenty-four years have elapsed since those of our brethren who arose in open revolt against the Federal Union, laid down their arms. Since that memorable time, hundreds of structures have been erected throughout the loyal States, in honor of the men who served their country on land or sea, during the terrible days of the civil war. Repeated projects and efforts to carry out a similar plan in honor of the men of Nashua, have failed of success until the present year, when it was reserved for the City Councils of 1889 to provide in behalf of the people of Nashua, for the erection of a suitable monument to perpetuate the memory of the Soldiers and Sailors of our city, who took their lives in their hands and went out from among us, in defense of their Country. Nashua's loyalty to the Union was exemplified by the large quota of volunteers from our midst, in response to the various calls of the government for men. From our farms, work-shops and factories—indeed, from all the pursuits, callings and professions of life, sprung forth recruits to battle for an imperilled Union. With all due respect to the honored members of the City Governments which have preceded us—it is with feelings of regret that I call attention to the fact, that the names of these brave men have never been enrolled upon the official records of our city. Unfortunately the State records and rosters pertaining to Nashua are incomplete and unreliable. Your committee have labored under great difficulties in making up the roll of honor to be deposited in this Corner-Stone. That roll of honor contains the names of 1355 men who were credited to Nashua's quota. The graves of about 275 of this number have to-day been strewn with flowers by the comrades of John G. Foster Post, and an unknown number sleep where they fell. "The structure to be erected on the solid foundations which are in position before you, will not be needed for the dead, the chief purpose of the admonishing sculpture will be to teach the living, in all coming time, lessons of patriotism and loyalty to country." May the monument to be erected stand through years of peace and plenty, not only adding new dignity to our fair city, but as a fitting emblem of a free government of a free people. We are here to-day to lay the Corner-Stone of that monument, and in the name and behalf of the honorable City Councils, and of the people of Nashua, by whom this structure is to be erected, I bid you all a hearty welcome.

5. Singing The National Anthem, "America," in Concert, by Pupils of the Public Schools of Nashua, under the direction of George E. Crafts.

6. Presentation of Dr. George W. Currier, Grand Master of Masons

of New Hampshire, by His Honor, the Mayor, with the request that the Corner-Stone be laid in accordance with the forms and usages of the Order of Free and Accepted Masons, as follows :—

Most Worshipful Grand Master of the Grand Masonic Lodge of New Hampshire :—

In response to an invitation extended to you in behalf of the citizens of Nashua, you are here to-day, attended by the distinguished officers and members of the fraternity, for the purpose of laying the Corner-Stone of a structure to be erected on these foundations, in honor of the Soldiers and Sailors of Nashua. As the chief magistrate of the city, and in the name and behalf of its citizens, it is my agreeable duty to ask you now to take charge of these ceremonies, and see that this Corner-Stone be laid in accordance with the time honored customs of the order.

The Grand Master replied as follows :—

Your Honor and Gentlemen of the Committee :—

It was with much pleasure that the Grand Lodge of Masons in New Hampshire accepted your kind invitation to lay the Corner-Stone of the structure here to be erected to perpetuate the memory of those brave men who went forth at their Country's call, with their lives in their hands, to maintain the supremacy of their Country's flag, on land and on sea, at home and abroad.

From time immemorial it has been the custom of the Fraternity of Free and Accepted Mason to assemble, when requested, upon the occasion of laying the Corner-Stone of any public structure, and perform certain ceremonies of the craft. In accordance with that time honored custom, I will now assume charge, and proceed with the ceremony, as provided by our Order.

7. Ceremony of Laying the Corner-Stone of the Soldiers' and Sailors' Monument by the Grand Lodge of Masons of New Hampshire.

The Grand Master addressed the assembly as follows:—

The teachings of Freemasonry inculcate, that in all our works, great and small, begun and finished, we should seek the aid of Almighty God. It is our first duty, then, to invoke the blessing of the great Architect of the Universe upon the work in which we are about to engage. I therefore command the utmost silence, and call upon all to unite with our Grand Chaplain in an address to the Throne of Grace.

PRAYER BY THE GRAND CHAPLAIN.

Almighty God! who hath given us grace at this time, with one accord, to make our common supplication unto Thee, and dost promise that where two or three are gathered together in Thy name, Thou wilt grant their request; fulfill now, O Lord! the desires and petitions of Thy servants, as may be most expedient for them; granting us in this world, knowledge of Thy truth; and in the world to come, life everlasting. Amen.

Response. So mote it be.

Grand Master. Right Worshipful Brother Grand Treasurer. it has ever been the custom on occasions like the present. to deposit within a cavity in the stone, placed in the north-east corner of the structure, certain memorials of the period at which it was erected; so that in the lapse of ages. if the fury of the elements, or the slow but certain ravages of time should lay bare its foundation, an enduring record may be found by succeeding generations, to bear testimony to the energy, industry and culture of our time. Has such a deposit been prepared?

(At this point, a box twelve inches long, eight inches wide, and eight inches high, made of thick plates of lead and secure-

ARTICLES DEPOSITED.

ly sealed, containing the articles to be deposited in the Corner-Stone, was handed to the Grand Treasurer by Charles S. Bussell, City Clerk of Nashua.)

Grand Treasurer. It has, Most Worshipful Grand Master, and the various articles of which it is composed are safely enclosed within the casket now before you.

Grand Master. Right Worthy Grand Secretary you will read for the information of the brethren and others here assembled, a record of the contents of the casket.

LIST OF ARTICLES DEPOSITED IN THE CORNER-STONE AS READ BY THE GRAND SECRETARY.

1. Certified copy of Resolution No. 978, providing for the erection of a Soldiers' and Sailors' Monument, passed January 29, 1889, and certified copy of Resolution No. 990, in relation to laying this Corner-Stone, passed May 28th, 1889.
2. Names of 1355 Nashua Soldiers and Sailors in the war of the Rebellion.
3. Autograph signature of the President of the United States.
4. Autograph signature of the Vice-President of the United States.
5. Autograph signature of the Governor of New Hampshire.
6. Deposit by John G. Foster Post, No. 7, G. A. R., containing list of all the soldiers who ever belonged to the Post; Members of the Woman's Relief Corps; Sons and Daughters of Veterans; a G. A. R. badge and copy of By-Laws of the Post.
7. Copy of City Charter and Revised Ordinances.
8. Copy of City Report, 1888.
9. Copy of Manual of City Officers, 1889.
10. Copy of Manual of School Board and Teachers of 1889.
11. Copy of Directory of City of Nashua, 1888.
12. Copy of Nashua *Weekly Gazette*, May 30th, 1889.
13. Copy of Nashua *Daily Gazette*, May 29th, 1889.
14. Copy of Nashua *Weekly Telegraph*, May 25th, 1889.
15. Copy of Nashua *Daily Telegraph*, May 29th, 1889.
16. Programme of the exercises at laying of this Corner-Stone.

ARTICLES DEPOSITED.

17. Deposit by the Nashua Fire Department.
18. Deposit by St. George Commandery, Knights Templar.
19. Deposit by Granite Lodge, No. 1, I. O. O. F.
20. Deposit by Pennichuck Lodge, No. 44, I. O. O. F.
21. Deposit by Nashoonon Encampment, I. O. O. F.
22. Deposit by Ancient Order of Hibernians, Divisions Nos. 1 and 2.
23. Deposit by Union St. Jean Baptiste Society.
24. Deposit by Conclave T. B. Crowley, Knights of Sherwood Forest, A. O. F.
25. Deposit by Women's Christian Temperance Union.
26. Roster of J. Q. A. Warren Camp, No. 18, Sons of Veterans.
27. Roster of Foster Rifles, Co. I, Second Regiment, N. H. N. G.
28. Silver and minor coins of the U. S., 1889.
29. Copies of Manchester *Daily Union*, Boston *Daily Journal, Herald* and *Globe*, May 30th, 1889.
30. Copy of the *Army and Navy Journal*, New York, May 4th, 1889.
31. Pamphlet descriptive of the Washington Centennary, celebrated in New York, April 29, 30 and May 1, 1889.

Grand Master. Right Worthy Grand Treasurer, you will now deposit the Casket beneath the Corner-Stone, and may the Great Architect of the Universe, in His wisdom, grant that ages on ages shall pass away ere it again be seen of men.

(The Grand Treasurer, assisted by the Grand Secretary placed the casket in the cavity prepared, the Second Regiment band playing softly during the ceremony.)

Grand Treasurer. Most Worshipful Grand Master, your orders have been duly executed.

(The principal architect here delivered the working tools to the Grand Master, who retained the trowel, and presented the square, level and plumb to the Deputy Grand Master, Senior and Junior Grand Wardens, respectively, and said) :—

Right Worshipful Brethren, you will receive the implements of your office. With your assistance and that of the Craft, I will now proceed to lay the Corner-Stone of this structure, according to the custom of our fraternity.

Brother Grand Marshal, you will direct the Craftsmen to furnish the cement, and prepare to lower the stone.

The Grand Master then spread the cement, and the stone was slowly lowered to its place, to the sound of appropriate music, the GRAND HONORS being given under the direction of the Grand Marshal. The Grand Master then said:—

Right Worthy Deputy Grand Master, what is the proper implement of your office?

Deputy Grand Master. The Square.

Grand Master. What are its moral and Masonic uses?

Deputy Grand Master. To square our actions by the rule of virtue, and prove our work.

Grand Master. Apply the implement of your office to that portion of the Corner-Stone, and make report.

The square is applied to the four upper corners.

Deputy Grand Master. Most Worshipful Grand Master, I find the stone to be square. The Craftsmen have done their duty.

Grand Master. Right Worthy Senior Grand Warden, what is the proper implement of your office?

Senior Grand Warden. The Level.

Grand Master. What are its moral and Masonic uses?

Senior Grand Warden. Morally, it teaches Equality; and by it we prove our work.

Grand Master. Apply the implement of your office to that portion of the Corner-Stone that needs to be proved, and make report.

The Level was applied to the top surface.

Senior Grand Warden. Most Worshipful Grand Master, I find the stone to be level. The Craftsmen have done their duty.

Grand Master. Right Worshipful Junior Grand Warden, what is the proper implement of your office?

Junior Grand Warden. The Plumb.

Grand Master. What are its moral and Masonic uses?

Junior Grand Warden. Morally it teaches rectitude of conduct; and by it we prove our work.

Grand Master. Apply the implement of your office to that portion of the Corner-Stone, and make report.

The Plumb was applied to the sides of the stone.

Junior Grand Warden. Most Worshipful Grand Master, I find the stone to be plumb. The Crafstmen have done their duty.

The Grand Master then struck the stone three times with his gavel and said:—

This Corner-Stone has been tested by the proper implements of Masonry. I find that the Craftsmen have skillfully and faithfully done their duty; and I do declare the stone to be well formed and trusty, truly laid, and correctly proved according to the rules of our Ancient Craft. May the structure be conducted and completed amid the blessings of Plenty, Health and Peace.

Response by the Craft. So mote it be.

Grand Master. Brother Grand Marshal, you will present the elements of consecration to the proper officers.

MASONIC CEREMONIES. 43

Grand Marshal presented Vessel of Corn to the D. G. M. ; the Wine to the S. G. W. ; and the Oil to the J. G. W.

Deputy Grand Master advanced with the Corn, scattered it on the stone, and said,

I scatter this Corn as an emblem of Plenty ; may the blessings of bounteous Heaven be showered upon us, and upon all like patriotic and important undertakings, and inspire the hearts of the people with virtue, wisdom and gratitude.

Response by the Craft. So mote it be.

Senior Grand Warden advanced with the Vessel of Wine, poured it on the stone, and said :—

I pour this Wine as an emblem of Joy and Gladness. May the Great Ruler of the Universe bless and prosper our National, State and City Governments ; preserve the union of the States in harmony and brotherly love, which shall endure through all time.

Response by the Craft. So mote it be.

Junior Grand Warden advanced with Vessel of Oil, poured it on the stone and said :—

I pour this Oil as an emblem of Peace ; may its blessings abide with us continually ; and may the Grand Master of Heaven and Earth shelter and protect the widow and orphan, and vouchsafe to them, and to the bereaved, the afflicted and sorrowing, everywhere, the enjoyment of every good and perfect gift.

Response by the Craft. So mote it be.

Grand Master extended his hands, and pronounced the following invocation :—

May Corn, Wine and Oil, and all the necessaries of life abound among men throughout the world. May the blessing of Almighty God be upon this undertaking. May he protect the workmen from every accident. May the monument here to be erected, be planned with WISDOM, supported by STRENGTH, and adorned in BEAUTY, and may it be preserved to the latest ages, a fitting tribute to the brave defenders of our country and a lasting monument to the liberality of our citizens.

Response by the Craft. So mote it be.

Grand Master addressed the Principal Architect and said:—

Worthy sir, having thus, as Grand Master of Masons, laid the Corner-Stone of this Monument, I now return to you these implements of operative Masonry, having full confidence in your skill and capacity to perform the important duties confided to you, to the satisfaction of those who have entrusted you with their fulfilment.

The Grand Master then made report of his doings as follows:—

I have the honor to report, that in compliance with the request of the proper authorities, the Corner-Stone of the Monument to be erected on this site, has been laid successfully, with the ancient ceremonies of the Craft. The Brother Grand Marshal will therefore make the proclamation.

Grand Marshal. In the name of the Most Worshipful Grand Lodge of Free and Accepted Masons of the State of New Hampshire, I now proclaim that the Corner-Stone of the Monument to be erected, has this day been found *true* and *trusty*, and laid according to the old customs, by the Grand Master of Masons.

8. Oration by Colonel Frank G. Noyes, of Nashua.

Mayor Burke then introduced the Orator of the Day, as follows :—

Ladies and Gentlemen :—

By invitation of the City Councils, one of our distinguished fellow citizens will now address you. This gentleman is too well-known to Nashua people to require any introduction. I therefore present to you Colonel Frank G. Noyes.

THE ORATION.

Mr. Mayor and Fellow Citizens:—

At the height of the grandeur and glory of Ancient Rome, it was said of her citizens that to be a Roman was greater than a king. We Americans are here to-day with a prouder title than could be justly assumed by any dweller in that Roman city, that "sat upon her seven hills and from her throne of beauty ruled the world." We are here as citizens of the Republic of free and independent United States of America. We are here in the name of Liberty and Union to perform a sacred ceremony. In the name of Liberty! that finds its springs and sources deep in the hearts of men. With all its beauty, with all its mistakes, its faith and inspiration, it belongs to no nation, no creed, no race. It is the heritage of man.—In the name of Union! that was founded by the Fathers of the Republic, and cemented by the blood of our fathers and brothers. It has received its "baptism of fire"; we have tested it in the crucible of civil war, and by the aid of those over whose mouldering bones, their surviving comrades have this day strewn the sweet flowers of spring, we have illustrated its deathless existence.

THE ORATION.

THE CORNER-STONE.

We are here to lay the Corner-Stone of a memorial structure to be erected by this city, as a tribute of honor to the men of Nashua who served their country on land or sea during the war of the rebellion, and aided in preserving the integrity of the Federal Union. While we engage in this solemn duty, we have here with us participating in these obligations, representatives of the battle-scarred heroes of the Grand Army of the Republic, as well as many other equally worthy veterans who survived the conflict, all of whom we delight to honor. To perform this grateful ceremony, we have invoked to our assistance an Ancient and Honorable Order, founded on the Christian religion; whose tenets inculcate loyalty to country; that claims an antiquity more remote than the dawn of the Christian era, and one of whose distinguished masters was the peerless Washington.

THE MONUMENT.

For the people of our day and generation, the deeds of the heroes in whose honor this structure is to be raised, need no illustration by tongue or pen, or pile of stone or bronze. They are imperishable and inshrined in the hearts of their countrymen. But to create and bequeath to the youth of future generations, a memorial of the sublime virtues of loyalty and patriotism, is a deed worthy of the intelligence of the most advanced civilization. To you, therefore, gentlemen of the City Councils, by whose wisdom this memorial structure is to be erected by the people of Nashua, in their name and behalf, I offer you thanks. In the name of the heroic dead whose faith and achievements you commemorate, I offer you thanks. In the name of their surviving comrades, I offer you thanks.

In the name of the youth of the present, and of future generations, I offer you thanks.

THE DEPOSIT.

We here deposit in this Corner-Stone, memorials of our day and age. In thus entombing these treasures, we consign to a long and silent repose, mementoes of ourselves that shall again behold the light, only when we, perchance, have been long forgotten; when perhaps our names would have passed into oblivion, and our existence have become a tradition, save only for the stately shaft that shall be erected on these foundations, to perpetuate the memory of those who offered their lives upon the altar of their country, and to be a constant, though silent reminder of their patriotism, heroism and devotion.

THE OCCASION.

During the brief time I shall address you to-day, I purpose to swerve from the somewhat beaten track that has usually been trodden by orators on similar occasions for the last quarter of a century. Those of you who are of mature age well remember, and the youth before me have heard by word of mouth or perusal of faithful histories, the thrilling incidents that occurred throughout the North, following the attack upon our Country's flag in '61. When the tocsin was sounded! When the toilers at the loom, the forge, and the anvil dropped their machines with the speed still on! when the farmer left his plough in the furrow! when the workmen in God's vineyard, whether from the presses of the shop, the counter, the office, the bench, or the pulpit, all laid down their implements of peaceful avocations, and girding on an unwonted armor, bade farewell to home and friends amid tears and prayers, and marched to defend the honor of the Republic! Well might you here listen to a recital of some reminiscences of that terrible period. Because we here stand on almost hallowed ground. Here about us I behold many reminders of those dark days of danger and doubt. Here I see on this platform a citizen of Nashua, esteemed in his advancing years as he was honored in his earlier manhood, who as Chief Magistrate [1] of the city, received the battered veterans of the war, as they returned victorious after Appomatox, and welcomed them home upon this very spot. But should we not endeavor to draw lessons of wisdom on this occasion, rather than indulge in reminiscences of the war?

The occasion is not and should not be one of unmixed grief. Its ceremonies furnish us with sources of pleasure as well as sad reflection. It is an appropriate time to examine our progress as a nation, to consider our present condition and the influence of our example, to extend our sympathies to other people engaged in the same struggle in which we have conquered, and above all to rekindle upon the altar of a common patriotism, such torches as have been quenched or grown dim amid party contests or attempted civil disunion.

THE SAFETY OF THE REPUBLIC.

The safety of our Republic is assured by the exercise of two inalienable rights; first, the free exercise of public opinion upon the public acts of the party in power; and second, co-equal with this public opinion, and its voice, the ballot box, that

> "Weapon that comes down as still
> As snow-flakes fall upon the sod;
> But executes the freeman's will,
> As lightning does the will of God." [2]

It is somewhat popular in these days of assumed modern political degeneracy, to smile at a suggestion of the purity of

---

[1]. Ex-Mayor V. C. Gilman.
[2]. John Pierpont.

our ballot box system. Subtle schemers and smooth tongued frauds, and sometimes men who " steal the livery of the Court of Heaven to serve the devil in,"[1] use their hellish devices to corrupt and pollute the fountains whence flow the pure waters of freedom; but as intelligence shall become diffused throughout the land, the masses of those men who now lie under the thick clouds and dead calm of ignorance, superstition and vice, will surge like the angry ocean, and the reign of terror to all such corruptionists, will be the history of the nation!

THE STRENGTH OF THE REPUBLIC.

The great strength of our Republic lies in the innate love of freedom and of country implanted in our people; the love of justice and fair play; the calm, sober second thought of our men and women, and such conditions of soil and climate as render the genius of our institutions capable of producing in cases of emergency, such men as Washington, Jefferson, Jackson and Lincoln. And above all, it is that ardent patriotism that rises above self. It is that electric fire of freedom which to-day is shaking the very foundations of kingdoms and empires. The handwriting is on the wall! What to-day do you plainly behold among the monarchies of the old world? " Change, change, change," written on everything; mysterious vials of wrath momentarily threatening to pour; the awful horseman of the Apocalypse crying out from the clouds,—" Behold I make all things new."[2] Every sceptre trembling in a palsied grasp; every crown fretted with sleeplessness and thorns; arms in the hands of soldiers sprung from the people, and who cannot be trusted to turn against them; secret societies filling the air with

---
1. Pollock's Course of Time.
2. The Revelation of St. John.

missiles of destruction from invisible hands, and Poland, Hungary and Ireland preparing for the inevitable hour, when a deadlier blast than Roland blew from his enchanted horn, shall summon them to take their places as free, sovereign and independent Commonwealths, around the standard of reconstructed Europe!

THE UNITY OF THE PEOPLE.

The great heart of our people, my fellow-citizens, has always throbbed with love of country; the rank and file whatever may be their party affiliations are all patriots. The issues of the war of the rebellion, settled forever the question of universal freedom in our country. Those of our brethren in the Southern States who rebelled, were arrayed against the Union in support of an *ignis fatuus* that lured them on almost to their destruction. But the masses in the South to-day, are as loyal to the Union as any of us here. The Boys in Blue and the Boys in Gray march under one flag now, the stars and the stripes of the Federal Union. The line reaches the length and breadth of the land, and it cannot be broken.

And so to-day our people are free, independent, prosperous and happy citizens of the grandest Republic the world has ever known; a Nation with such resources and so united and powerful, that it might successfully withstand the world in arms. Let us therefore beware of the dangers that threaten us; beware of the allurements of luxury; beware of the concentration of wealth by means of gigantic trusts, combinations and other devices which menace the liberties of the people; of the tendency to centralization of power by which all the Republics in the past have been overthrown; resist every encroachment on the autonomy of the States, and yield no iota of their vested rights. Thus may the Republic endure forever!

THE FUTURE OF THE REPUBLIC.

We have briefly considered the present; let us now look to the future:—Within the next century I behold my countrymen numbering three hundred millions of freemen! I see the whole continent under her starry flag! I see her the center of civilization! Thrones have tottered and crumbled, and dynasties have been swept away! I see her at the zenith, full orbed, "glittering like the morning star, full of life, and splendor, and joy." [1]

9. Benediction by the Grand Chaplain of the Grand Lodge of Masons, as follows:—

Glory be to God on High, and on earth, peace, good will toward men! O Lord, we most heartily beseech Thee with Thy favor to behold and bless this assemblage; pour down Thy mercies, like the dew that falls upon the mountains, upon Thy servants engaged in the solemn ceremonies of this day. Bless, we pray Thee, all the workmen who shall be engaged in the erection of this monument; keep them from all forms of accident and harm; grant them in health and prosperity to live; and finally, we hope after this life, through Thy mercy and forgiveness to attain everlasting joy and felicity in Thy bright mansion, in Thy holy temple, not made with hands, eternal in the heavens. Amen.

Response. So mote it be.

At the close of the exercises at Abbot Square, the column moved down Main Street, by the City Hall Building, where it was reviewed by the Mayor and City Government, thence countermarched to the starting point, where the parade was dismissed.

---

[1]. Edmund Burke.

SECOND REPORT OF BUILDING COMMITTEE.

REPORT OF THE BUILDING COMMITTEE.

NASHUA, N. H., SEPT. 17, 1889.

To THE CITY COUNCILS :—

GENTLEMEN :—Your Committee appointed under the provisions of joint resolution Number 978, entitled :—" A Resolution for the erection of a Soldiers' Monument, and appropriation not exceeding twelve thousand dollars," passed January 29th, 1889, begs leave respectfully to again report progress and state,

First :—That the contractors for building the Monument have given this Committee formal notice that the same will be finished and ready for dedication on the 15th day of October, next.

Second :—That this Committee is, therefore, making arrangements to have the Monument dedicated with appropriate ceremonies on said 15th of October.

Third :—That the Commander of the Grand Army of the Republic for the Department of New Hampshire, has been invited and has accepted the invitation to perform the ceremony of dedication, assisted by the comrades of the order.

Fourth :—That the Hon. Charles H. Burns, of Wilton, has been invited and has accepted the invitation to deliver an oration on the occasion.

Fifth :—That your Committee did not feel authorized nor warranted to trespass on the rights and dignity of your honorable bodies so far as to ask or appoint any member of the City

Councils to serve on any of the Committees to attend to the details of arranging for the dedication of the Monument, but your Committee begs respectfully to suggest that your honorable bodies take such action as may seem advisable, to act as a General Committee of Reception to the guests of the City on that occasion.

Your Committee further begs respectfully to suggest that your honorable bodies take such action as you may deem proper, to be present officially on the occasion of the dedication of the Monument, on Abbot Square, at the time stated above.

Your Committee begs respectfully to request that your honorable bodies will ratify the action of your Committee in the premises, by accepting this report.

Respectfully submitted,

CHARLES H. BURKE,
  Mayor and Chairman,
JOHN D. SULLIVAN,
A. W. HEALD,
H. P. WARDWELL,
J. H. MORAN,
CHARLES W. STEVENS,
FRANK G. NOYES,
R. B. PRESCOTT,
  Secretary,

Building Committee of the Soldiers' Monument.

Received Sept. 30, 1889.

Read and accepted in Board of Aldermen, Oct. 1st, 1889.

    CHARLES H. BURKE, Mayor.
    CHARLES S. BUSSELL, City Clerk.

Read and accepted in Board of Common Council, Oct. 1st, 1889.

    HENRY P. WHITNEY, President,
    GEORGE E. DANFORTH, Clerk.

ARRANGEMENTS FOR THE DEDICATION.

ARRANGEMENTS FOR THE DEDICATION.

As soon as the Building Committee were assured by the contractors that the Monument would be finished and ready for dedication within the time specified in the contract, preparations were begun and arrangements made for a ceremony and pageant that should be worthy of the object, and the fifteenth of October, 1889, was set as the day on which to dedicate the Monument.

The Committee invited the following named persons to take part in the dedicatory services:—

The Commander of the Grand Army of the Republic for the Department of New Hampshire, assisted by his staff and comrades of the order, to dedicate the Monument.

Hon. Charles H. Burns of Wilton, to deliver the oration.

Rev. Geo. W. Grover to act as chaplain.

Colonel Frank G. Noyes in behalf of the Building Committee, to formally deliver the Monument to the City.

Col. E. J. Copp to act as Chief Marshal.

These invitations were severally accepted.

Invitations to participate in the ceremonies were forwarded to every Grand Army Post in New Hampshire, and to several Posts in adjoining States. A circular was published in all the newspapers in the State, extending to all soldiers and sailors who were either born in, or were credited to, or now reside in New Hampshire, who have served in the army or navy of the

ARRANGEMENTS FOR DEDICATION.

United States, a cordial invitation to be present and take part on the occasion of unveiling and dedicating the Monument.

A general committee of arrangements was appointed, consisting of the following named citizens:—

> Mayor Charles H. Burke, Chairman,
> Hon. Frank A. McKean,
> Hon. James H. Tolles,
> Gen. Ira Cross,
> W. D. Cadwell, Esq.,
> Col. E. J. Copp,
> Dr. A. W. Petit,
> Col. Frank G. Noyes,
> Alvin S. Eaton, Esq.,
> Charles W. Stevens, Esq.,
> Patrick Lonergan, Esq.,
> Dr. R. B. Prescott, Secretary.

There were also appointed sub-committees on invitation, on entertainment, on transportation, on order of exercises and printing, on decorations, on music, on carriages, and a large reception committee consisting of ex-mayors and other prominent citizens.

The members of both branches of the City Government also acted as a special committee on reception.

All the committees, comprising more than an hundred citizens labored earnestly, industriously and in entire harmony throughout the whole affair, and with the sole object of making the occasion a grand success, a credit and an honor to the city.

The following General Orders were issued by the Chief Marshal :—

GENERAL ORDERS.

Dedication of the Soldiers' and Sailors' Monument.
Office of Chief Marshal.
Nashua, N. H., Sept. 25, 1889.

Orders No. 1.

I. Having been appointed Chief Marshal of the exercises at the dedication of the Soldiers' and Sailors' Monument at Nashua, October 15th next, the undersigned hereby assumes the duties of the office.

The following appointments are hereby announced :—

Dr. R. B. Prescott, Chief of Staff.
Col. Dana W. King, Assistant Marshal and Chief of Division.
H. A. Marsh, Assistant Marshal and Chief of Division.
C. W. Stevens, Assistant Marshal and Chief of Division.
M. A. Taylor, Assistant Marshal and Chief of Division.

AIDS.

Col. R. P. Staniels of Concord,	Col. J. J. Dillon of Manchester,
Col. John B. Hall of Manchester,	Col. F. E. Kaley of Milford,
Col. W. E. Spalding of Nashua,	Capt. G. E. Heath of Nashua,
Maj. W. H. Cheever of Nashua,	Capt. M. L. Morrison, Peterboro',
Capt. W. W. Hemmenway, Milford,	Dr. G. F. Wilbur of Nashua,
Adjt. C. E. Faxon of Nashua,	J. H. Dunlap of Nashua,
Capt. F. L. Kimball of Nashua,	Capt. C. E. Nelson of Derby Line,
Capt. D. B. Newhall of Concord,	W. A. Gregg of Nashua,
Loren S. Richardson of Concord,	C. H. Moore of Nashua,
J. A. Dadman of Concord,	John H. Vickery of Nashua,
G. F. Hammond of Nashua,	P. Lonergan of Nashua,
F. E. Marsh of Nashua,	Darius Whithed of Lowell,
L. P. A. Lavoie of Nashua,	John Welch of Lowell,
Col. J. W. Crosby of Milford,	Daniel Walker of Lowell,
B. S. Woods of Nashua,	D. W. Hayden of Hollis.

II. Chiefs of Division and Aids will report at 9 o'clock, A. M., Oct. 15, at the Office of Chief Marshal, County Building.

III. John G. Foster Post, G. A. R., will report to the Chief Marshal for special escort duty at 10 o'clock, A. M.

Companies I. and C., Second Regiment, N. H. N. G., having volunteered their services for the day, unless otherwise ordered, will report to the Chief Marshal for special escort duty at 10 o'clock, A. M.

IV. All visiting organizations will report upon arrival to the Assistant Marshal or Aid in waiting at each station.

V. Dinner will be served at 12 o'clock on North Common to the Military, to the visiting organizations of the G. A. R., and to all Soldiers and Sailors of the war who may favor us with their presence.

VI. Lines will be formed at 1:30 P. M. by Divisions under direction of Chiefs of Division as follows:—

First Division upon the westerly side of Main street, with the right resting upon Factory street.

Second Division upon Temple street, with the right resting upon Main street.

Third Division upon East Pearl street, with the right resting upon Main street.

Fourth Division upon Main street, with the right resting upon Hollis street.

The line of March will be as follows: Main street to Belmont street, countermarch through Main to Concord street, Concord street to Courtland, countermarch Courtland to Crescent, Crescent to Abbot, Abbot to Abbot Square.

VII. The formation of Divisions and assignment of command, with other details, will be announced in future orders.

VIII. All organizations intending to participate, that have not already reported, are urgently requested to communicate with the Chief Marshal without delay. The co-operation of all Soldiers and prompt compliance with orders is absolutely necessary to the success of the ceremonies.

E. J. COPP, Chief Marshal.

DEDICATION OF THE SOLDIERS' AND SAILORS' MONUMENT.
OFFICE OF CHIEF MARSHAL,
NASHUA, N. H., OCT. 10, 1889.

ORDERS No. 2.

I. So much of paragraph No. VI of Orders No. 1 from these headquarters as relates to the time of formation of line is hereby revoked. Lines will be formed by Divisions under the direction of Chiefs of Divisions at 1 o'clock P. M., Oct. 15th.

First Division upon westerly side of Main street, with the right resting at Factory street.

Second Division upon Temple street, with the right upon Main street.

Third Division upon East Pearl street, with the right upon Main street.

Fourth Division upon Main street, with the right upon Hollis street.

GENERAL ORDERS.   63

II. The column will move at 1:30 o'clock in the order named below, through Main street to Belmont street, countermarch through Main to Concord street, Concord street to Courtland street, Courtland street to Webster street, Webster street to Hall street, Hall to Concord, Concord to Crescent, Crescent to Abbot, Abbot to Abbot Square.

* * * * * * * *

(The Column or line of Procession which follows here in the General Order, is given hereinafter beginning on page 83.)

* * * * * * * *

All organizations not having yet reported will be assigned to position in line in the order in which they report.

Col. D. W. King will establish headquarters upon the Oval, Railroad Square, to whom all Veterans unattached to organizations, will report at or before 11 o'clock A. M. and will be organized by him into a Veterans' Division.

All organizations arriving early in the day will reassemble upon the ground upon which they break ranks, at 11 o'clock preparatory to marching to the North Common for dinner. To obtain admittance to the dining tent, it will be necessary for Soldiers and Veterans to appear with their organizations under the command of Col. King, as above directed.

Immediately following dinner, Post Commanders will conduct their commands to the point of Division formation, reporting to the Chief of the Division to which they are assigned.

VI. Capt. S. S. Piper, commanding First Light Battery, N. H. N. G., is charged with the firing of the National Salute of 42 guns upon the unveiling of the Monument. For this purpose he will place his battery in position on North Common, and upon orders transmitted by the Signal Corps will fire the salute.

VII. Upon the termination of the ceremonies, commanders of visiting organizations will reform their lines and march to the depot for embarkation. The Chief Marshal in command suggests that every man in line appear with sufficient underclothing to make the wearing of an overcoat unnecessary.

It is confidently expected that every man participating in the ceremonies of the day will place himself under reasonable discipline, obeying all orders promptly. Every soldier knows this to be necessary to success.

By order of
E. J. COPP, Chief Marshal.

Official,
R. B. PRESCOTT, Chief of Staff.

The following General Orders were issued from Grand Army headquarters :—

HEADQUARTERS DEPARTMENT OF NEW HAMPSHIRE,
GRAND ARMY OF THE REPUBLIC.
CONCORD, AUG. 6, 1889.

GENERAL ORDERS,
No. 6.

* * * * * * * *

IV. The Department officers have accepted an invitation extended by the city of Nashua, N. H., to dedicate a Soldiers' and Sailors' Monument in that city, October 15, 1889, and a cordial invitation is extended to all of the Posts in this Department to be present and participate in the ceremonies. Post Commanders are requested to bring this subject before their respective Posts for their action, at the first meeting of their Posts after receiving this order, and will notify (by letter) Col. E. J. Copp, Chief Marshal, of their acceptance and the probable number of comrades that will be present. They will also report to Col. Copp upon their arrival in Nashua on the day specified, for assignment to position in column.

V. The Commander of John G. Foster Post, No. 7, will detail one comrade to act as Officer of the Day, one comrade to act as Officer of the Guard, and six comrades (three soldiers and three sailors) to act as Guard of Honor, and report their names to the Assistant Adjutant General immediately.

VI. The Department Commander is assured that the various railroads in the state will issue round trip tickets at the lowest possible rates, which will soon be published; and it is hoped that the comrades will avail themselves of this opportunity, turn out out with full ranks, and pay honor to the memory of the heroic dead.

VII. If the date of the dedication of the monument should be changed, due notice will be given.

By command of

J. F. GRIMES, Department Commander.

JAMES MINOT, Assistant Adjutant-General.

GENERAL ORDERS.

Headquarters Department of New Hampshire,
Grand Army of the Republic.
Concord, Sept. 23, 1889.

General Orders,
No. 9.

I. Post Commanders are reminded that the time fixed—October 15th—for the dedication of the Soldiers' and Sailors' Monument at the city of Nashua, N. H., is near at hand, and as they are to be the guests of the city upon that occasion, it is *very essential* that they report their acceptance or non-acceptance of the invitation, with the probable number that will be present, by letter, as directed by Section IV of General Orders No. 6 from these Headquarters, in order that the city may know the number for which to provide entertainment. Posts that have not so reported will do so at once.

II. A collation will be served to the comrades as near 12 o'clock M. as possible and the dedicatory exercises will commence about 2 o'clock P. M., and close in season to allow the comrades to return to their homes, that night, if they desire.

III. The Concord, Cheshire, Boston & Maine, Old Colony, and Fitchburg Railroads, and leased lines, have agreed to carry passengers at 1 1-2 cents per mile, and in no case shall the fare exceed three dollars for the round trip whatever the distance may be.

Tickets will be on sale at all the principal stations, and good going to Nashua on the 14th and 15th and returning on the 15th and 16th days of October.

IV. All the Staff Officers are cordially invited to be present at the dedication and will notify the Assistant Adjutant General of their acceptance by letter without delay.

V. The following named officers are directed to report to the Department Commander at Nashua, N. H., as early as practicable on the day of the dedication and take the respective parts assigned them in the dedicatory exercises:—

Thomas Cogswell, Senior Vice Dep't Commander.

George E. Hodgdon, Junior Vice Dep't Commander.

James K. Ewer, Chaplain.

James Minot, Assistant Adjutant-General.

VI. Comrades G. F. Bailey and J. L. Burgess, of Post No. 7, G. A. R., are hereby detailed as Officer of the Day and Officer of the Guard, respectively, and will report to the Assistant

Adjutant-General for duty at 1 o'clock P. M. on the day of the dedication.

By command of

J. F. GRIMES, Department Commander.

JAMES MINOT, Assistant Adjutant-General.

THE MONUMENT.

THE MONUMENT.

The Monument is an imposing structure, and as a creation of memorial art, for beauty of design and appropriate expression to commemorate the deeds of the men whose memories it is intended to perpetuate, has seldom been equalled.

The Monument is located near the south east corner of Abbot Square, at the head of Main street, and far to the south, beyond the City Hall Building, the view is unobstructed.

It is built of granite and is as solid and should endure as the very hills themselves. The foundation is of solid masonry eleven feet below the surface of the earth. The base is fifteen feet and six inches square and the Monument is fifty-two feet and eight inches in height, with castellated shaft. The main die is hammered and the blocks forming the column alternate hammered and rough ashler, the contrast being perfect. The inscription on the bronze tablet on the South face of the die is:—

A TRIBUTE
TO THE MEN OF NASHUA
WHO SERVED THEIR COUNTRY
ON LAND OR SEA
DURING THE WAR OF THE REBELLION,
AND AIDED IN
PRESERVING THE INTEGRITY
OF THE
FEDERAL UNION
A. D. 1861–1865.

ERECTED BY THE CITY OF NASHUA
A. D. 1889.

On this side of the die, above the inscription, in bronze and tastefully grouped, are the emblems of the cavalry arm of the service. The group consists of a saddle, thrown carelessly against a stone wall, upon which is a hat and blanket; upon the side and below are the canteen, sword, rifle, straps, pistol and other trappings, with a bugle lying upon the ground at the left.

The tablet on the North face of the die is given to appropriate quotations, as follows:—

"THE UNION OUGHT TO BE CONSIDERED AS A MAIN PROP OF YOUR LIBERTIES, AND THE LOVE OF THE ONE OUGHT TO ENDEAR TO YOU THE PRESERVATION OF THE OTHER."—[WASHINGTON'S FAREWELL ADDRESS.

"OUR FEDERAL UNION; IT MUST BE PRESERVED."—[ANDREW JACKSON.

"LIBERTY AND UNION, NOW AND FOREVER, ONE AND INSEPARABLE."—[DANIEL WEBSTER.

"THAT FROM THESE HONORED DEAD WE TAKE INCREASED DEVOTION TO THAT CAUSE FOR WHICH THEY GAVE THE LAST FULL MEASURE OF DEVOTION; THAT WE HERE HIGHLY RESOLVE THAT THESE DEAD SHALL NOT HAVE DIED IN VAIN AND THAT GOVERNMENT OF THE PEOPLE, BY THE PEOPLE, FOR THE PEOPLE, SHALL NOT PERISH FROM THE EARTH.—[ABRAHAM LINCOLN.

"LET US HAVE PEACE."—[U. S. GRANT.

The bronze emblem above the inscriptions on this side of the die consists of a group of three cannon, with an artillery wheel below and two rammers perpendicular.

THE MONUMENT. 71

The bas-relief, in bronze, upon the East face of the die, represents the sinking of the Alabama by the Kearsarge, June 19, 1864, off the coast of France. The Alabama is engulfed, sinking in the sea, while the victorious Kearsarge is seen in the background, on even keel, seemingly uninjured by the fight. Above, on the top of the die, stands a bold and defiant sailor in bronze, 7 feet 2 inches in height. His right arm is extended above his head; his right hand grasps a cutlass, his left hand holding a rope, a coil of which lays at his feet. The idea conveyed is that he is about to board an enemy's ship. The band upon his hat is inscribed "Kearsarge." The appropriateness of this tablet and figure is found in the fact that the victorious war ship bore the name of a New Hampshire mountain and is therefore identified with this State. It is also found in the fact that the last male descendant of Matthew Thornton, the signer of the Declaration of Independence, Capt. James S. Thornton, whose body lies buried at Thornton's Ferry, was the executive officer of the Kearsarge in the memorable engagement, and directed the guns that brought victory and honor to his country.

The bas-relief upon the West face of the die is allegorical and of special significance. The capitol of the nation appears upon the right background and a ruined Southern dwelling house upon the left, in front of which stands a stack of muskets, resting upon which is a furled rebel flag. The Goddess of Liberty, with broken chains at her feet and with outstretched hands, stands in the center; before her in kneeling attitude is a colored man over whose head a Federal and Confederate soldier have clasped hands in the bonds of peace, while a ribbon border across the top and bottom bears the inscription: "With malice toward none; with charity for all." Upon the top of this side of the die stands a spirited figure, in bronze, of an infantryman in the act of raising and cocking his rifle. The figure, upon which is a haversack, cartridge-box and canteen, leans forward ; the gaze is intently fixed on a far away object, while every nerve is strained to the utmost tension. The thought of the beholder instantly grasps the idea that the soldier is represented, either as a skirmisher, or on a lonely picket line, and that an important movement of the enemy is being watched with absorbing interest. We doubt if the figures of the soldier and sailor of this Monument are equalled by any in this country. Equalled or excelled, they are perfect works of art and a credit to artist and committee.

On the four sides of the capstone of the shaft, there are four bronze shields ; the one upon the South face is a copy of the seal of the State ; that upon the North, a copy of the seal of the City, and those upon the East and West are copies of the United States shield. The stone is ornamented with columns at the corners and with raised stars at the top.

Standing upon a pedestal of proper proportions and crowning the whole, is a statue representing Victory. It is nine feet high and carved from New Hampshire Granite. Its symmetry is perfect. The features are beautiful ; firm, yet benign ; the drapery flowing and graceful in folds ; the effect perfect in art. The right hand rests upon the symbolic shield of the country, and the extended left holds a laurel wreath in bronze.

This Monument has been erected to commemorate the patriotism and valor of the thirteen hundred and fifty-five men of Nashua, who served their Country as Soldiers or Sailors during the War of the Rebellion, whose names are deposited in the Corner-Stone It is a worthy and appropriate tribute to the living and dead of the army and navy of the Union. and when it shall have been improved by adding statues of a cavalryman and artilleryman in bronze, in place of the emblems now upon the North and South faces of the second die, there

THE MONUMENT. 73

will be no Monument in our country—at whatever cost—that will more appropriately mark the greatest epoch liberty has ever known.

NOTE.—The design and general plan of the Monument was made by Mr. T. M. Perry, Architect for Messrs. Frederick & Field of Quincy, Mass. The model of the Sailor was made by S. J. O'Kelly, sculptor, of Boston, and was cast by M. H. Mosman, of Chicopee, Mass. The model of the Skirmisher (the soldier) was made by C. Buberl, of New York, and was cast by the Henry Bonnard Bronze Co., of New York. The model of the Artillery emblem was made and the same was cast by M. H. Mosman, of Chicopee, Mass., who also furnished the model of the Emancipation bas-relief and the two lettered panels, and cast the same. The model of the Cavalry emblem, the bas-relief of the sinking of the Alabama, City Seals and U. S. shields, and the surmounting Statue of Victory were modelled by Beattie & Brooks, sculptors, Quincy, Mass. The Cavalry emblem and Naval bas-relief were cast by Henry Bonnard Bronze Co., of N.Y. The City Seals and U. S. Shields were cast by M. H. Mosman, of Chicopee, Mass. The surmounting figure of Victory, carved from a block of Concord, N. H., granite, was executed in the works of Messrs. Frederick & Field, by their own sculptors. All the granite work of the Monument was executed in the works of the contractors and builders, Messrs. Frederick & Field, of Quincy, Mass., who erected the Monument. The foundation of the Monument—which is eleven feet deep, and fifteen feet and six inches square at the top, and flares regularly to the bottom, where it is eighteen feet square—is built from granite raised from the Nashua quarry, and was laid by Charles W. Stevens, of Nashua, under the direction of Frederick & Field. The dedicatory inscription on the bronze tablet inserted in the south or front face of the die of the Monument, and the quotations from eminent Americans, on the bronze tablet inserted in the north face of the same, were prepared by Col. Frank G. Noyes, of Nashua.

THE DAY.

THE DAY.

The fifteenth day of October, 1889.

It was a perfect autumn day, bright and beautiful. The air was cool and bracing. It was the day to which the people of Nashua had looked forward for nearly a quarter of a century; the day on which a Monument was to be dedicated to the memory of sons and brothers, of husbands and fathers, who, in the pride and strength of their manhood, went forth to battle for the integrity of the nation as a federal union; which should set the bondman free and preserve the liberties of the people. The city was decked in its finest raiment. Public and private buildings were elaborately decorated with flags and banners and bunting, and hundreds of beautiful and ingenious devices, which testified to the patriotic feeling and general interest which the public had in the grand event. It was surely Veterans' day. The factories closed, business suspended, the streets crowded with people, the assemblage of many distinguished personages to do honor to the occasion, the gathering together of more than three thousand veterans of the war who were comrades on weary marches, lonely bivouacs and bloody fields, irresistably turned the mind back more than a quarter of a century to a time when the whole nation swayed and staggered under the mighty power of civil war; when far away under the Southern sun, the true-hearted "boys in blue" were giving their lives to protect those institutions that were priceless heirlooms to the loyal northern heart. Nashua in tender remembrance, had called together her sons and daughters to do honor to those heroes and their surviving comrades.

Before eight o'clock, hundreds of vehicles that brought visitors from the suburbs and the adjoining towns were upon the streets, and the highways were thronged with thousands of pedestrians.

The arrival of the early railway trains brought large delegations, and when the later trains came rolling in, they were literally burdened with loads of war veterans and people from the cities and towns of the State and Massachusetts, and invited guests from places both near and remote. The visiting Grand Army Posts, Veteran Soldiers and Sailors unattached, the Military and other organizations, and invited guests were received and welcomed upon their arrival at the several railroad stations by special committees of citizens, and escorted to the various rendezvous. The veterans, the military and other organized bodies were then " off duty " until the call for dinner. All other specially invited guests were escorted to the City Hall, where the Mayor and members of the City Councils and the general committee on reception warmly welcomed them.

Provision had been made to organize a Division composed of veterans who should be present, unattached to any post or other organization. Col. Dana W. King was assigned to duty, as chief of this Division. He established a rendezvous at the park in Railroad Square, and appointed special aids, with instructions to attend the arrival of all railroad trains, and otherwise to scour the city in search of recruits, to enlist for the day and march under the flag of this old veteran's division. This resulted in the gathering at the rendezvous of more than an hundred grizzled veterans who were heartily welcomed, and were gratified that Nashua had provided a place for them, although nearly all had come to town as strangers. Col. King organized them as a battalion, which comprised in its ranks many men of eminence, among whom were a Past Department Commander of Maine and many others of equal rank who had served their country on land or sea. After dining with the thousands on the North Common, this batallion was assigned to a place in the line on the right of the fourth division. The Lisbon Drum Corps, 22 pieces, Bailey, leader, which played martial music after the manner of fifty years ago marched proudly at the head of this unique command.

Twelve o'clock, noon, was announced in general orders as the hour for dinner. Preparation had been made to entertain all guests of the city with dinner and other needed refreshments. The committee on entertainment had made ample provision to furnish "a square meal" to every old soldier and sailor in Nashua on that day,—whether in or out of the Grand Army of the Republic—to all the Military, and to all the Sons of Veterans present. Two Yale tents of the largest size were pitched on the North Common, and in these tents, between the hours of twelve and one o'clock, forty-five hundred men partook of an abundant dinner. The rations consisted of baked beans, beef, ham, and tongue, brown and white bread, doughnuts, pickles, fruit and coffee, and all in ample supply.

The Mayor in behalf of the City Government had issued cards of invitation to his excellency the Governor and Staff, to the members of the Governor's Council, the Judges of the Supreme Court, the Commander of the Grand Army of the Republic of the Department of New Hampshire, and staff, the Brigade Commander and the field and staff officers of the New Hampshire National Guard, the New Hampshire delegation in Congress and many other distinguished guests, to partake of a complimentary luncheon at the Tremont House, at 12 M., noon. At this feast, upwards of two hundred guests of the city were entertained.

Some of the visitors were invited to the homes of friends in the city; others were cared for at the hotels, and it is safe to say that no guest of the city on that day was unprovided with ample, hearty and satifactory entertainment.

Meanwhile the streets were thronged with a multitude of people, and all seemed supremely happy.

THE PROCESSION.

THE PROCESSION.

At one o'clock, P. M., lines were formed by Divisions under the direction of Chiefs of Divisions, as announced in General Orders and were as follows :—

First Division upon westerly side of Main street, with right resting at Factory street.

Second Division upon Temple street, right resting upon Main street.

Third Division upon East Pearl street, with right resting upon Main street.

Fourth Division upon Main street, with right resting upon Hollis street.

Half-past one o'clock in the afternoon was the appointed time for the column to move. As soon as the several divisions were formed, the order to march was sounded, and the procession moved in the order given below :—

Through Main street to Belmont street, thence countermarching through Main to Concord street, Concord street to Courtland street, Courtland street to Webster street, Webster street to Hall street, Hall street to Concord street, Concord street to Crescent street, Crescent street to Abbot street, Abbot street to Abbot Square.

Assistant City Marshal, W. W. Wheeler.
Platoon of Eight Policemen.
Chief Marshal, Col. E. J. Copp.
Chief of Staff, Dr. R. B. Prescott.

MARSHALS AND AIDS.

Col. R. P. Staniels of Concord,
Col. John B. Hall of Manchester,
Col. W. E. Spalding of Nashua,
Col. J. W. Crosby of Milford,
Maj. W. H. Cheever of Nashua,
Adjt. C. E. Faxon of Nashua,
Lieut. G. P. Kimball of Nashua,
Dr. C. S. Collins of Nashua,
G. F. Hammond of Nashua,
F. E. Marsh of Nashua,
L. P. A. Lavoie of Nashua,
B. S. Woods of Nashua,
Col. J. J. Dillon of Manchester,
Col. F. E. Kaley of Milford,

Col. H. M. Goodrich of Nashua,
Capt. M. L. Morrison, Peterboro',
Dr. G. F. Wilbur of Nashua,
W. A. Gregg of Nashua,
J. H. Dunlap of Nashua,
Capt. C. E. Nelson of Derby Line,
John H. Vickery of Nashua,
P. Lonergan of Nashua,
Darius Whithed of Lowell,
John Welch of Lowell,
Daniel Walker of Lowell,
D. W. Hayden of Hollis,
C. H. Moore of Nashua,
Arthur D. Ramsdell of Nashua.

SIGNAL CORPS.

FIRST DIVISION.

SECOND REGIMENT BAND, N. H. N. G., W. A. Cummings, bandmaster.
FIRST BRIGADE, NEW HAMPSHIRE NATIONAL GUARD,
Brig.-Gen, J. N. Patterson, Commanding.

STAFF.

Lieut.-Col. George W. Gould, Assistant Adjutant-General,
Major Albert N. Dow, Assistant Inspector General,
Major Harry B. Cilley, Inspector of Rifle Practice.
Major Frank W. Rollins, Judge Advocate,
Captain Daniel H. Gienty, Aid-de-Camp,
Captain Frank L. Kimball, Aid-de-Camp,
Brig. Color Sergeant, Arthur H. Knowlton.

SECOND REGIMENT, NEW HAMPSHIRE NATIONAL GUARD,
Col. A. W. Metcalf, Commanding.

Lieut.-Col. Jason E. Tolles,
Major Francis O. Nims,
First Lieut. Sumner Nims, Adjutant,
First Lieut. E. W. Emerson, Quartermaster,
Captain C. A. Roby, Paymaster,
Major George W. Flagg, Surgeon,
Captain William H. Nute, Assistant-Surgeon,
Captain Henry B. Smith, Chaplain.

Sergeant Major E. P. Whitney, Quartermaster Sergeant G. E. Danforth, Commissary Sergeant, F. H. Weeks, Hospital Steward, G. C. Shedd, Drum Major, S. M. Hoyt. Color Sergeant D. P. Barker, Band Master W. A. Cummings.

Foster Rifles, Co. I. E. H. Parmenter, captain; W. H. Goodspeed, first lieutenant; W. R. Seaman, second lieutenant.

Smith Rifles, Co. K, of Hillsborough Bridge. L. E. Nichols, captain; John W. Craine, first lieutenant; Homer A. White, second lieutenant.

Keene Light Guard, Co. H. J. P. Wellman, captain; Frank Chapman, first lieutenant: E. A. Shaw, second lieutenant.

Keene Light Guard, Co. G. Charles W. Starkey, captain; E. O. Upham, first lieutenant; Charles E. Joslin, second lieutenant.

Company C, of Nashua. Hiram S. Stevens, captain; Arthur D. Farley, first lieutenant; William H. Livingstone, second lieutenant.

MANCHESTER BATTALION OF INFANTRY.
Col. G. M. L. Lane, Commanding.

DRUM CORPS of Company K, First Regiment. N. H. N. G. Six men.
Col. G. M. L. Lane.
Major P. A. Devine,
Acting Adjutant, First Lieut. J. F. Reardon,
Quartermaster Sergeant, T. E. F. McDerby,

Sheridan Guards, Co. B, First Regiment, N. H. N. G. D. F. Shea, captain; J. F. Reardon, first lieutenant; William Sullivan, second lieutenant.

City Guards, Co. E, First Regiment. N. H. N. G. B. N. Wilson, captain; Frank W. Tibbitts, first lientenant; John B. Rogers, second lieutenant.

THE PROCESSION.

Manchester High School Cadets. W. Parker, captain; A. W. Morgan, first lieutenant; A. F. Wheat, second lieutenant.

Lafayette Guards, Co. H, First Regiment, N. H. N. G. Jeremie H. Soley, first lieutenant; Frank H. Lussier, second lieutenant.

Company K, of Manchester, First Regiment, N. H. N. G. P. H. O'Malley, captain; T. H. Kendrigan, first lieutenant, John Fitzmorice, second lieutenant.

DETACHMENT THIRD REGIMENT, NEW HAMPSHIRE NATIONAL GUARD.

Maj. William A. Messer, Commanding.

Weston Guards, Co. D, Pittsfield, Walter Langmaid, first lieutenant; commanding; Delta H. Merrill, second lieutenant.

State Capital Guards, Co. C, Concord, William C. Trenoweth, captain; H. B. Roby, first lieutenant; Thomas P. Davis, second lieutenant.

MANCHESTER CORNET BAND, J. D. Ricord, leader.

Amoskeag Veterans, Major E. F. Trow, Commanding; Captain John B. Abbot, Adjutant.

Manchester Cadets, Frank L. Downs, captain; Ed. T. Knowlton, first lieutenant; Ed. R. Robinson, second lieutenant.

Nashua High School Cadets, R. S. Wason, captain; M. W. Mitchell, first lieutenant; W. S. Williams, second lieutenant.

HIS EXCELLENCY THE GOVERNOR OF NEW HAMPSHIRE, AND STAFF, (Mounted.)

His Excellency, DAVID H. GOODELL, Governor,

Maj-Gen. Augustus D. Ayling, Adjutant-General, Concord,

Brig.-Gen. Elbert Wheeler, Inspector-General, Nashua,

Brig.-General Charles O. Hurlbut, Quartermaster-General, Lebanon,

Brig.-Gen. Sylvester Little, Commissary-General, Antrim,

Brig.-Gen. John H. Cutler, Surgeon-General, Peterborough,

Col. Fred A. Palmer, Aide-de-Camp, Derry Depot,

Col. Daniel F. Healy, Aide-de-Camp, Manchester,

Col. Stephen S. Jewett, Aide-de-Camp, Laconia,

Col. Edward M. Gilman, Aide-de-Camp, Nashua.

THE PROCESSION.

First Light Battery, N. H. N. G.
Samuel S. Piper, Captain,
Edward H. Currier, First Lieutenant,
Silas R. Wallace. First Lieutenant,
John A. Barker, Second Lieutenant.

SECOND DIVISION.

Dunstable Cornet Band, C. W. Spalding, leader.
Captain Charles W. Stevens, Chief of Division, and Staff.
John G. Foster Post, No. 7, G. A. R., Nashua, Alfred Chase, commander.
General J. G. Foster Post, No. 163, G. A. R., South Framingham, Mass., William F. Brown, commander.

Worcester Cornet Band.

George A. Ward Post, No. 10, G. A. R., Worcester, Mass., A. M. Parker, commander.
General Lander Post, No. 5, G. A. R., Lynn, Mass., Eli W. Hall, commander.
Major Howe Post, No. 17, G. A. R., Haverhill, Mass., ——————— commander.

Lowell Cornet Band.

B. F. Butler Post. No. 42. G. A. R., Lowell, Mass., Charles A. R. Dimon, commander.

Cornet Band.

James A. Garfield, Post, No. 120, G. A. R., Lowell, Mass., L. A. French, commander.

Cornet Band.

Ladd and Whitney Post, No. 185. G. A. R., Lowell, Mass., Franklin S. Pevey, commander.
E. S. Clark Post. No. 115, G. A. R., Groton, Mass., John S. Hartwell, commander.
George S. Boutwell Post, No. 48, G. A. R., Ayer, Mass., George L. Sawyer, commander.
Thomas A. Parker, Post, No. 195, G. A. R., Pepperell. Mass.. George H. Morrill, commander.

Old Concord Post, No. 180, G. A. R., Concord, Mass., George F. Wheeler, commander.

Edwin V. Sumner Post, No. 19, G. A. R., Fitchburg, Mass., Charles H. Glazier, commander.

THIRD DIVISION.

MILFORD CORNET BAND, D. Arthur Vittum, leader.

Captain M. A. Taylor, Chief of Division, and Staff.

Oliver W. Lull Post, No. 11, G. A. R., Milford, N. H., H. F. Warren, commander.

Louis Bell Post, No. 3, G. A. R., Manchester, N. H., Charles A. Frost, commander.

Willard K. Cobb Post, No. 29, G. A. R., Pittsfield, N. H., John M. Gilman, commander.

Stover Post, No. 1, G. A. R., Portsmouth, N. H., B. Stowe Laskey, commander.

DOVER CORNET BAND.

C. W. Sawyer Post, No. 17, G. A. R., Dover, N. H., William Drew, commander.

E. E. Sturtevant Post, No. 2, G. A. R., Concord, N. H., E. H. Dixon, commander.

William I. Brown Post, No. 31, G. A. R., Penacook, N. H., D. E. Jones, commander.

Bell Post, No. 74, G. A. R., Chester, N. H., A. D. Emery, commander.

A. A. Livermore Post, No. 71, G. A. R., Wilton, N. H., H. L. Emerson, commander.

G. H. Phelps Post, No. 13, G. A. R., Amherst, N. H., Cyrus Cross, commander.

Upton Post, No. 45, G. A. R., Derry, N. H., W. H. Thomas, commander.

Wesley D. Knight Post, No. 41, G. A. R., Londonderry, N. H., W. P. Nevins, commander.

PETERBOROUGH CORNET BAND.

Aaron F. Stevens Post, No. 6, G. A. R., Peterborough, N. H., Charles R. Peaslee, commander.

J. H. Worcester Post, No. 30, G. A. R., Hollis, N. H., Isaac W. Pierce, commander.

THE PROCESSION.

E. N. Taft Post, No. 19, G. A. R., Winchester, N. H., John W. Hammond, commander.

Harvey Holt Post, No. 15, Lyndeborough, N. H., Jason Holt, commander.

Gilman E. Sleeper Post, No. 60, G. A. R., Salem, N. H.. C. E. Conant, commander.

Stark Fellows Post, No. 46, G. A. R., Weare, N. H., A. F. Page, commander.

Herman Shedd Post, No. 27, G. A. R., Greenville, N. H., Thomas E. Marshall, commander.

HILLSBOROUGH CORNET BAND.

Senator Grimes Post, No. 25, G. A. R., Hillsborough Bridge, N. H., E. L. Carr, commander.

Ephraim Weston Post, No. 89, G. A. R., Antrim, N. H., Leander Emery, commander.

John Sedgwick Post, No. 4, G. A. R., Keene, N. H., Walter W. Glazier, commander.

FREMONT CADET BAND.

Joe Hooker Post, No. 51, G. A. R., Fremont, N. H., David W. Coffin, commander.

Col. Putnam Post, No. 5, G. A. R., Hopkinton, N. H., Sylvester W. Perry, commander.

Davis Post, No. 44, G. A. R., West Concord, N. H., Abiel C. Abbott, commander.

—— —— Post, No. —, G. A. R., Danville, N. H.. David B. Cumer, commander.

FOURTH DIVISION.

LISBON DRUM CORPS, Twenty-two Men, —— Bailey, leader.

Captain George E. Heath, Chief of Division and Staff.

Division of Veterans, (Soldiers and Sailors unattached,) Col. Dana W. King, commanding.

Lieutenant-Colonel, Natt Shackford,

Major, Captain Charles E. Buzzell,

Adjutant, Eri Oaks.

Sons of Veterans, Col. B. O. Roby, commanding.

90   *THE PROCESSION.*

J. Q. A. Warren Camp, No. 18, Sons of Veterans. George E. Cross, captain; Eugene H. Paige, first lieutenant; James H. Thornton, second lieutenant.

CIVIC ORGANIZATIONS.

Ancient Order of Hibernians, Division No. 1. John M. Lee, president; Patrick Lonergan, marshal; Patrick E. Moran, assistant marshal.

Union St. Jean Baptiste Society. E. D. Perrault, president; Dorilla Cardin, marshal; Rev. J. B. H. V. Millette and Rev. H. A. Lessard, chaplains.

Ancient Order of Hibernians, Division No. 2. J. J. Doyle, president; —————— Marshal.

CITY GOVERNMENT AND INVITED GUESTS, as follows:

Barouche containing His Honor, Charles H. Burke, Mayor; Hon. Charles H. Burns, Orator of the Day; Rev. G. W. Grover, Chaplain; Col. J. W. Grimes, Commander of the Grand Army of the Republic, Department of New Hampshire.

Barouche containing Col. Thomas Cogswell, Senior Vice-Commander, G. A. R., Department of New Hampshire; Hon. George E. Hodgdon, Junior Vice-Commander, G. A. R., Department of New Hampshire; Rev. J. R. Wilkins, Acting-Chaplain, G. A. R., Department of New Hampshire; James Minot, Assistant Adjutant-General, G. A. R., Department of New Hampshire.

Barouche containing Isaac W. Hammond, Assistant Quartermaster General, G. A. R., Department of New Hampshire; Liberty W. Foskett, Inspector, G. A. R., Department of New Hampshire; Col. Daniel Hall, Judge Advocate, G. A. R., Department of New Hampshire; William H. Tripp, Chief Mustering Officer, G. A. R., Department of New Hampshire.

Barouches containing the members of the Board of Aldermen of the City of Nashua.

Barouches containing the members of the Common Council of the City of Nashua.

Barouche containing T. M. Perry, Architect, and Messrs. Frederick & Field, Contractors, and R. A. Maxfield, Esq.

Barouche containing the Building Committee of the Monument.

THE PROCESSION. 91

Barouche containing the Mayors of Concord, Manchester, Dover and Keene.

Barouches containing Ex-Mayors of Nashua: Honorables V. C. Gilman, G. H. Whitney, S. D. Chandler, F. A. McKean, Charles Holman, A. M. Norton, J. A. Spalding and James H. Tolles.

Barouche containing Ex-Mayor Dr. Edward Spalding; Hon. Isaac W. Smith, Associate Justice of the Supreme Court of New Hampshire; Ex-Governor Frederick Smyth, and Ex-Governor P. C. Cheney.

Barouche containing Ex-Governor B. F. Prescott; Ex-Governor Moody Currier; Gen. D. M. White, and Col. Thomas G. Banks.

Barouche containing members of Governor's Council, Hons. Charles H. Horton; Edward C. Shirley; William S. Pillsbury, Frank C. Churchill, and Hon. David A. Gregg.

Barouche containing United States Senator Henry W. Blair; Congressmen Alonzo Nute and Orren C. Moore; and E. S. Cutter, Esq.

Barouche containing Ex-Congressmen M. A. Haynes, Dr. J. H. Gallinger. Luther F. McKinney; and W. W. Bailey, Esq.

Barouche containing Major A. B. Thompson, Secretary of State of New Hampshire; Solon A. Carter. State Treasurer; Hon. J. W. Patterson, Superintendent of Public Instruction, and Major Archibald H. Dunlap.

Barouche containing Gen. S. G. Griffin, Gen. M. T. Donahoe, Col. Babbitt (9th N. H. Vols.) and Col. Hapgood, (5th N. H. Vols.)

Barouche containing Gen. E. S. Greeley; Mr. Charles P. Clark, (late Commander, U. S. N.) Col. French and Col. H. M. Putney, (chairman Board of Railway Commissioners for New Hampshire.)

Barouche containing Hon. Mark F. Burns (Ex-Mayor of Somerville, Mass.), Hon. George A. Marden, of Lowell; H. A. Barton, Esq., and Hon. E. P. Brown.

Barouche containing Hon. Sam. W. Dickinson, George W. Burke, Esq., A. N. Flinn, Esq., and John Field, Esq.

Barouche containing Ex-Department Commanders. G. A. R., of New Hampshire, James E. Larkin, William H. Trickey, T. W. Challis and Alvin S. Eaton.

Barouche containing Ex-Department Commanders, G. A. R., of New Hampshire, John C. Linehan, Marcus N. Collis. George Farr, and Otis C. Wyatt.

Barouche containing Hon. Henry D. Upton, Speaker of House of Representatives of New Hampshire; Capt. D. B. Newhall; Capt. W. K. Norton, and Hon. E. O. Blunt.

Barouche containing Hon. D. A. Taggart, President of the Senate of New Hampshire; Thomas D. Luce, Esq., Clerk of the Supreme Court of Hillsborough County; Capt. Charles D. Copp, and Mr. O. Williams, Superintendent of Public Schools, Nashua.

Barouches containing Representatives of the Press.

Barouches containing members of the General Committee of Arrangements; Committee on Entertainment; Committee on Invitation; Committee on Order of Exercises and Printing; Committee on Transportation; Committee on Decorations; Committee on Music; Committee on Carriages, and Committee on Reception.

Other Guests in Carriages.

Citizens in Carriages.

THE DEDICATION.

THE DEDICATION.

A raised platform or grand stand which seated nearly a thousand people was erected on the South side, or front, of the Monument, on Abbot Square.

Admission to this platform was by ticket, in the distribution of which especial effort was made to furnish them to widows and female relatives of soldiers and sailors who have joined the silent majority, and to the families of living veterans.

On this platform were seated, besides those above mentioned, the members of the City Government, the Governor's Council, State Officers, ex-Governors of the State, Judges of the Supreme Court, the Congressional Delegation from New Hampshire, Mayors of New Hampshire cities, United States Government officials, Past Commanders and other Past Department officers of the G. A. R. for New Hampshire. Nashua veterans residing outside the State, representatives of the press, and other distinguished guests.

Another and smaller stand was erected on the west side of the Monument, on which were seated the Governor and Staff, the Commander of the Grand Army of the Republic and Staff, the Orator, the Chaplain of the Day, the Mayor of Nashua and the Building Committee of the Monument.

The ceremonies were in the following order :—

DEDICATION

OF THE

SOLDIERS' AND SAILORS' MONUMENT.

NASHUA, N. H., OCTOBER 15, 1889.

PROGRAMME AT ABBOT SQUARE.

(At 3 o'clock, p. m.)

1. ANNOUNCEMENT by His Honor, Chas. H. Burke, Mayor of Nashua.

2. INVOCATION by the Chaplain of the Day, Rev. G. W. Grover.

3. UNVEILING THE MONUMENT, by Miss Jennie Josephine Chase, six years of age, daughter of the Commander of J. G. Foster Post No. 7, G. A. R., and

    DELIVERY OF THE MONUMENT to the City in behalf of the Building Committee, by Col. Frank G. Noyes.

    (Following the unveiling of the Monument a National Salute was fired from the North Common by the 1st Battery, N. H. N. G., Capt. S. S. Piper Commanding.)

4. ADDRESS UPON RECEIVING THE MONUMENT in behalf of City, by His Honor, the Mayor.

5. NATIONAL ANTHEM, "America," sung by the audience, led by the Second Regiment Band, N. H. N. G.

> My country! 'tis of thee
> Sweet land of liberty
>   Of thee I sing;
> Land where my fathers died
> Land of the pilgrim's pride;
> From ev'ry mountain side.
>   Let freedom ring.
>
> My native country! thee—
> Land of the noble free,
>   Thy name I love:
> I love thy rocks and rills,
> Thy woods and templed hills,
> My heart with rapture thrills,
>   Like that above.
>
> Let music swell the breeze
> And ring from all the trees
>   Sweet freedom's song;
> Let mortal tongues awake.
> Let all that breathe partake,
> Let rocks their silence break,
>   The sound prolong.

THE DEDICATION.

6. PRESENTATION OF COL. JAMES F. GRIMES, Commander of the Grand Army of the Republic for the Department of New Hampshire, by His Honor, the Mayor, with the request that the Monument be dedicated in accordance with the ritual of the Order of the Grand Army.
7. DEDICATION OF THE MONUMENT by the Department Commander and Staff of the Grand Army of the Republic, assisted by the comrades of the Order.
8. ORATION by Hon. Charles H. Burns of Wilton.
9. BENEDICTION by the Acting Chaplain of the G. A. R. for the Department of New Hampshire, Rev. E. R. Wilkins, of Concord.

UNVEILING OF THE MONUMENT, AND ITS FORMAL DELIVERY TO THE CITY.

Upon arriving at Abbot Square, the column of procession was broken and massed around the Monument by the Chief Marshal.

The audience was called to order by Mayor Burke, who briefly announced the object of the occasion.

The Mayor then introduced the Chaplain of the Day, Rev. George W. Grover, who invoked the blessing of Deity.

The Building Committee of the Monument then arose, advanced to the front of the stand before the Mayor, and Colonel Frank G. Noyes in their behalf, formally delivered the Monument to the City.

Colonel Noyes spoke as follows:—

Your Honor, the Mayor of Nashua:—

By the instruction and in the name and behalf of the committee to whom was delegated by the City Councils of Nashua, the duty and power to carry out the provisions of a resolution authorizing the building of a Soldiers' and Sailors' Monument by the people of this city, I announce to you, sir, as its chief magistrate, that our labors are ended, our work is done. Before you, behold the result!

[At this point the Monument was unveiled by Miss Jennie J. Chase, six years of age, daughter of Commander Chase of Post 7, amid the booming of artillery, ringing of bells, music from the bands and general hurrahs from the thousands assembled, and a salute of 42 guns was fired from the North Common by the First Light Battery, N. H. N. G., Capt. S. S. Piper, commanding.]

Colonel Noyes then continued :—

It only remains for the committee to surrender to the city the product of their labor. Therefore, by authority of the Building committee here present, to you, sir, as the legal and proper representative of the City of Nashua, I now deliver this Monument. Receive it, sir, as free from stain and we trust as enduring, as are the deeds of the men whose memories it is intended to perpetuate.

MAYOR BURKE'S ADDRESS.

Mayor Burke then accepted the Monument in behalf of the City, and addressed the people as follows :—

Gentlemen of the Building Committee and Fellow Citizens :—

As Mayor, it becomes my duty as well as pleasure, to receive in behalf of the City of Nashua, from your hands, this beautiful and enduring memorial erected by our grateful city as a tribute to her sons who perilled their lives in their country's cause, and which is now to be dedicated with appropriate ceremonies.

Gentlemen of the Building Committee, it gives me pleasure to thank you in behalf of the City Councils and the citizens generally, for the faithful discharge of the high trust confided to you, and for the unceasing and untiring labors that have brought forth this Monument,—the consummation of months of earnest effort,—which reveals to-day one of the most noble and artistic memorial structures ever erected within the borders of our State.

Nearly a quarter of a century has elapsed since the close of the civil war, " harvests wave on its battlefields and time has obliterated its forts and trenches and softened the prejudices and passions kindled by the strife."

To the stranger within our gates it may seem that Nashua at this late day has been tardy in fulfilling the patriotic and sacred duty in here marking, in appropriate form, her sentiments of gratitude to her citizen soldiers.

Shortly after the close of the war of the rebellion, the City Government voted an appropriation of $12,000 to commemorate the gallant deeds of its sons in that contest, but in consequence of a great diversity of opinion and the lack of unanimity on the part of our citizens as to the location, or as to whether a Monument or a Memorial Hall should be built, the matter was deferred, and although agitated and discussed from time to time, no definite action was taken until the present year, when it was reserved for the City Councils of 1889, which I have the honor to represent, to provide for and locate upon this historic square, the structure now before us. A fitting and a worthy tribute to the brave men and the great sacrifices they made for the preservation of the Union! A Monument that will be a lasting ornament to the City. You have made it of granite and bronze, that it may withstand the ravages of time, and teach to one generation after another lessons of loyalty and patriotism.

Upon its top you have erected, carved in solid granite from the quarries of New Hampshire, a statue representing Victory, with a crown upon her head which denotes the supremacy of the government; her right hand rests upon the United States shield, and in her left hand she holds a laurel wreath, which are emblematic of triumph, peace, and the end of sectional strife. The bronze statues of heroic size and in active attitude, and the emblems, which collectively represent the principal divisions of the service of the army and navy, are original and of artistic merit.

Upon the four sides of the base of the pedestal are bronze bas-reliefs,—that upon the West representing, in plastic art, scenes and incidents that illustrate well, in a simple manner, the fruits of the victory in the greatest struggle for human rights the world has ever known.

That upon the East portrays the naval engagement between the United States sloop of war Kearsarge and the notorious and dreaded Confederate cruiser Alabama. Famous as is this battle throughout the world, it is especially memorable to us, from the fact that the Kearsarge was named for one of the mountains of the old Granite State, and also because one of Nashua's bravest sons was the executive officer of the victorious vessel in that conflict that dragged down the rebel flag, and sent the arrogant corsair ship to the bottom of the Atlantic, off the coast of France. The inscription on the South face of the Monument proclaims it to be erected as "A tribute of honor to the men of Nashua who served their country on land or sea during the war of the rebellion and aided in preserving the integrity of the Federal Union." This inscription, simple in language, is an impressive and fitting expression of the public appreciation of the brave deeds of the living and dead.

Upon the North side, in raised letters of polished bronze are inscribed famous expressions touching the union of the States, uttered by the lips of some of the nation's heroes and greatest men, from the days when the fathers of the Republic laid the foundation of our government, down to the present decade. There they will be read and pondered by those who succeed us, and in the history of our country they are recorded and will be remembered long after this Monument, with its soldier and sailor of bronze, shall perhaps have crumbled and become a shapeless mass.

Fellow Citizens: May we hope that with the completion of this long deferred but just tribute to Nashua's sons, our city has emerged from a comparatively inert past into an active, enterprising and expanding present, an epoch of wise progress in the community, a period of material prosperity that shall mark the beginning of the best and grandest history in the life of our city.

Living under the best form of government in the history of the world, let us cherish the hope that those who are to come after us may look back, over the track of centuries past, upon the Monument we now erect as the memorial of a still united and happy country.

THE DEDICATORY EXERCISES.

Mayor Burke then addressed Commander Grimes as follows:—

Commander Grimes of the Grand Army of the Republic for the Department of New Hampshire.

Mr. Commander :—

You have gratified and honored the people of Nashua by appearing here accompanied by the distinguished veteran officers and comrades who compose your command, in response to an invitation extended to you by our municipal councils to perform the solemn ceremony of dedicating this Monument, erected to honor the men of Nashua who served their country on land or sea during the war of the rebellion and aided in preserving the integrity of the Federal Union.

It is therefore my agreeable duty to ask you now to assume the direction of affairs, so that the good work may be accomplish in accordance with the ritual of the order of the Grand Army of the Republic.

Commander James F. Grimes gracefully accepted the invitation to dedicate the Monument and proceeded with the ritual of the order, being assisted by the Senior Vice Commander Thomas Cogswell ; Junior Vice Commander George E. Hodgdon ; Rev. E. R. Wilkins and Acting Chaplain, Officer of the Day G. F. Bailey.

Col. Grimes spoke as follows :—

Mr. Mayor :—

In the name of my comrades of the Grand Army of the Republic, representing as they do all soldiers and sailors who defended the integrity and authority of the nation, I thank you and those whom you represent for this memorial shaft. Its very silence is impressive. Without articulate speech, it is eloquent. It needs no words. It is itself an oration. It assures us that our dead are kept in remembrance,—those dead who gave their lives for the security of the citizens and the union of the states. It is significant of brave and loyal obedience to the command of the nation always and everywhere, since the obligations of citizenship are not restricted to time or place or to conflict of arms. It gives encouragement for the future, since the recognition and approval it gives of patriotic fidelity and heroism will be an incentive for the display of public valor and virtue in all coming time. There can be no doubt, sir, that the honor you pay to the patriot dead, and to their memorable deeds, will serve not only to make American citizenship in these days more reputable, but also to maintain and perpetuate, through all future generations the union and authority of the United States of America.

Adjutant, you will detail a guard of honor.

[The Adjutant called the following names: James A. Reed, James L. Burgess, James Blood and A. C. Gordon, on the part of the soldiers, and Edwin H. Webster, C. H. Holden, and William Nelson on the part of the sailors,—each man as his name was called, answering "Here."]

Adjutant.—Commander, the guard is present.

Commander.—Officer of the Day, you will direct the Officer of the Guard to station this detail about the memorial shaft.

Commander.—Holy Scripture saith :—

The Lord gave the word : great was the army of those that publish it. Ps. lxviii, ii.

Declare ye among the nations and publish and set up a standard. Jer. i. 2.

In the name of our God we will set up our banners. Ps. xx. 5.

Officer of the Day, you will order the Guard of Honor to display our flag.

Officer of the Day.—Officer of the Guard, let the flag be displayed.

Music—Band. "Star Spangled Banner."

Commander.—The forces of the Nation are divided into two great arms, that of the navy and that of the army. Senior Vice-Commander, what word of the Holy Scripture may apply to the

NAVY?

Senior Vice-Commander.—They that go down to the sea in ships, that do business in great waters, these see all the works of the Lord and His wonders in the deep. For He commandeth and raiseth the stormy wind, which lifteth up the waves thereof. Then they cry unto the Lord in their trouble, and He bringeth them out of their distresses. He maketh the storm a calm, so that the waves thereof are still. Then are they glad because they be quiet, so He bringeth them unto their desired haven. Oh, that men would praise the Lord for His goodness, and for His wonderful works to the children of men. Ps. cvii, 23, 24, 28-32.

Commander.—Officer of the Day, let the Guard of Honor set up the symbol of the navy, and let a sailor be detailed to guard it.

[An anchor was then set up against the shaft, crossed with a cutlass and boarding-pike. A comrade, dressed as a sailor, stood guard with drawn cutlass.]

Commander.—Junior Vice-Commander, what scripture may apply to the

ARMY?

Junior Vice-Commander.—To your tents, O Israel. So all Israel went to their tents.—2 Chron. x. 16. The children of Israel shall pitch their tents, every man by his own camp, and every man by his own standard, throughout their hosts.—Num. i. 52. Thou hast given a banner to them that fear thee, that it may be displayed because of the truth.—Ps. LX. 4. The Lord shall utter His voice before His army; for His camp is very great; for he is strong that executeth His word; for the day of the Lord is great and very terrible; and who can abide it?—Joel ii, 11. Some trust in chariots and some in horses; but we will remember the name of the Lord our God. Ps. xx. 7.

Commander.—Officer of the Day, let the Guard of Honor

THE DEDICATORY EXERCISES. 105

set up the symbol of the Army, and let a soldier be detailed to guard it.

[A musket with fixed bayonet, canteen and haversack hanging from it, knapsack leaning against the stock, was set up against the shaft opposite to the anchor. A comrade in full soldier uniform, armed with a musket with fixed bayonet stood guard.]

Commander.—Officer of the Day, if the work of navy and army be well done, what proclamation from Holy Scripture can you make?

Officer of the Day.—A proclamation of peace.

Lord, Thou wilt ordain peace for us: for Thou also hath wrought all our works in us.—Isaiah xxvi, 12. How beautiful upon the mountains are the feet of Him that bringeth good tidings, that publisheth peace, that bringeth good tidings, that publisheth salvation; that sayeth unto Zion, thy God reigneth. The Lord hath made bare His holy arm in the eyes of all the nations; and all the ends of the earth shall see the salvation of our God. Isaiah LII, 7, 10.

Commander.—The Chaplain will now offer the prayer of dedication.

Chaplain.—Almighty God, we thank Thee for Thy sovereign care and protection, in that Thou didst lead us in the days that were shadowed with trouble, and gavest us strength when the burden was heavy upon us, and gavest us courage and guidance so that after the conflict we have come to these days of peace. We thank Thee that the wrath of war has been stilled, that brother no longer strives against brother, that once again we have one country and one flag.

May Thy blessing be upon us as a people, that we may be Thy people, true and righteous in all ways, tender and patient in our charity, though resolute for the right; careful more for the down-trodden than for ourselves, eager to forward the interests of every citizen throughout the land, so that our country may be indeed one country from the rivers to the seas, from the mountains to the plains.

We pray Thee to make our memories steadfast, that we may never forget the generous sacrifices made for our country. May our dead be enshrined in our hearts. May their graves be the altars of our grateful and reverential patriotism.

And now, O God, bless Thou this memorial!

Bless it, O God, in honor of mothers, who bade their sons do brave deeds:

In honor of wives who wept for husbands who should never come back again:

In honor of children whose heritage is their fallen fathers' heroic name:

In honor of men and women who ministered to the hurt and dying:

But chiefly, O God, in honor of men, who counted not their lives dear when their country needed them, of those alike who sleep beside the dust of their kindred or under the salt sea, or in nameless graves, where only Thine angels stand sentinels till the reveille of the resurrection morning. Protect it and let it endure, and unto the latest generation may its influence be for the education of the citizen, for the honor of civil life, for the advancement of the nation, for the blessing of humanity, and for the furtherance of Thy holy kingdom.

Hear us, O our God, we ask it in the name of Him who made proof of the dignity and who consecrated the power of sacrifice in His blessed life and death, even in the name of Jesus Christ, the great Captain of our salvation. Amen.

Comrades.—Amen.

THE ORATION.

Commander.—Attention! Comrades of the Grand Army of the Republic.

In the name of the Grand Army of the Republic, I now dedicate this Monument. I dedicate it to the memory of those who in the navy guarded our inland seas and ocean coasts, and fell in defence of the flag. I dedicate it to the memory of those who in the army fought for our hillsides and valleys and plains and fell in the defence of the flag. I dedicate it to the memory of those brave and gallant men of our Army and Navy, who from '61 to '65, left their homes, their families, their friends and everything they held near and dear, buckled on the armor of war and went forth to do battle in defence of the Nation's honor that the Nation might live, and fell in defence of the flag.

Comrades, salute our dead!

Commander.—Attention! At ease.

Commander.—Mr. Mayor, our service of dedication is ended. In the name of my comrades I thank you and those who are associated with you, for your courtesy in giving us, who are bound by special ties to them, the privilege of dedicating this Monument, erected to perpetuate the memory of the heroic deeds of the Soldiers and Sailors of Nashua, (both living and dead) who fought upon land and sea during the war of the Rebellion.

At this point, the Mayor called the attention of the audience and introduced as the Orator of the Day, the HON. CHARLES H. BURNS, of Wilton, who then delivered the following

ORATION.

Mr. Mayor and Fellow Citizens:—

" Out of monuments * * * we doe save and recover somewhat from the deluge of time."—*Lord Bacon.*

For the first time in the history of the city of Nashua have its people assembled to dedicate a Monument to the everlasting honor of its dead and living heroes, whose brave work, on sea and land, is now a part of the imperishable story of our national struggles. Here it stands, on the historic spot from which they went forth to battle, freighted with the hopes and the fears and farewells of their fellow men, and to which they were welcomed after peace had been restored, with its back toward the unequalled Merrimack, "along whose smooth margin the ashes of our forefathers are laid," with its right to the "cloud-capped granite hills" of New Hampshire, and its left almost touching the borders of the grand old commonweath of Massachusetts, and its face toward a loving city, whose undying gratitude finds but feeble expression in this cold, silent, and yet suggestive, monumental shaft.

Its erection is in accordance with a time-honored custom prevailing among our own and other civilized nations; a custom dating so far back, that the "memory of man runneth not to the contrary." From almost the very dawn of creation traces of monuments which were evidently the work of man have been found. There seems to have been an instinct, born in the human breast, to erect something that should remain. The pyramids of Egypt, the mausoleums containing the bodies of distinguished dead, intended to defy the assaults of time; the tablets and monuments erected with marvelous industry throughout the ages, revealing an infinite variety of designs and objects; ancient hieroglyphics, cut mountain high, all bear test to the ever present desire to perpetuate in some enduring way, the deeds and heroism, the accomplishments and the sacrifices, of the human race. Away up among the Arctic snows, amidst eternal ice, Elisha Kent Kane, at great labor, built a pyramid of heavy stones, perched upon a mighty cliff, looking out upon "the icy desert," on which he placed the words " Advance 1853

-54," and surmounted it with the Christian symbol of the cross. He did it to remind those who might come after him that he had gone before. He did it to symbolize the hope and faith, that there would yet be established, in the midst of the ignorance and the stupidity and gloom of the frozen north, the power, the beauty, the sunshine, and the consolation of the Christian religion.

All over our land, a grateful people, following this touching instinct and custom, have constructed testimonials of their solemn appreciation of the inestimable work of the patriots, who saved this nation from the impending ruin of a rebellion, which was never before equalled in the life of nations, and to suppress which, more lives were lost than have been sacrificed in all the wars of all the nations of the old world since Waterloo, a period of seventy-five years. Almost every village and hamlet in the North, can point to its memorial, thus perpetuating, so far as possible, as sublime and patriotic incidents and events as ever graced the history of any nation known to man. The now historic battlefield at Gettysburg, where was fought one of the bloodiest and most stupendous battles of the world, and which was once covered with the slain of two mighty armies, is now dotted all over with monuments erected by the survivors and friends of those who died that the nation might live.

Not only have we placed testimonials to the valor of our glorious sons, exhibited on almost numberless battlefields, and in great naval wars, for the suppression of the Rebellion, but the people of our country, have from the closing moment of the great revolution, made manly efforts to erect, and have erected, noble structures, commemorating in many instances, in a striking manner, the great heroism and unselfish patriotism of our forefathers, in their mighty struggle to release the American people from the avarice and the tyranny of the people of Great Britain. Among the greatest of them all is that matchless granite shaft at Bunker Hill. It may not be as poetic a pile as some in Europe; it may not be as majestic as our great national monument at Washington; it may not be as historic as the statue of Liberty which has just been dedicated at "Plymouth the land of the Pilgrims," which commemorates events which adorn, with the bewitchery of romance, and the sternness of cold reality, the struggles, the sufferings, the sacrifices, and the achievements of that God-like band of noble souls who were the pioneers of the nation; but, reminding us, as this sublime monument does, of the opening scenes of the Revolution, and of an era in the history of our country when almost every man was a soldier; of the hour when the minute men of New England, left the plough in the furrow, seized the musket, and without further preparation, began the struggle for liberty in their own dooryards; and of the fact, that the brave sons of our own New Hampshire, were first on the consecrated spot to initiate a battle, which might determine whether or not, there should be a nation of freemen established on this continent, the shaft at Bunker Hill fills us with emotions, not inspired by any other monument on the face of the globe; and, added to all this, there is another fact which makes it peculiarly dear to every native of New Hampshire. At the laying of its corner-stone in 1825, by Lafayette, then the nation's guest, and when it was finally completed and dedicated years afterwards, New Hampshire's greatest son, Daniel Webster, spoke words of living and patriotic truth, which will abide when the granite of which it is made, shall have been dissolved into dust and have been lost in the sea that rolls at its base.

Nothing is so interesting to man as man. The chief charm of history is the light it throws upon the people of other days.

A chair in which a Washington sat, a table on which a Shakespeare wrote, a garment worn by some departed hero, a temple or monument commemorative of noble deeds, are objects of intense interest; the objects themselves are trifling, but the associations which cluster around them, the events they have witnessed or suggest, are important, and thrill with emotion the beholder who delights to go back in memory and learn something of the experiences and the deeds of those who have lived in another generation. There is an invisible chain connecting the man dead with the man living. There is a bond of sympathy between the life that has been and that which now is. Life would be comparatively worthless if it left no abiding influence behind, and whatever exemplifies or discloses this influence is precious. Out in Oregon, there are trees as huge and apparently as old as the cedars of Lebanon, but they do not attract equal attention with the grand old cedars, because they have no known history connected with the human race. Jerusalem, with its narrow streets and dingy buildings; a city without commerce, business, or beauty, would be wholly unattractive, were it not for the religious associations surrounding it. It was the city of David, and the Holy Sepulchre is there, and thousands traverse the globe, that they may sit and reflect within the shadows of its grim, historic walls. Damascus, the oldest city in the world, which was powerful in the days of Abraham, now has no attractions except in its fallen greatness and the strength it once possessed. Men spend their lives in exploring the earth for the ruins of cities, long since sunk from the light of day, that they may find in their buried bosoms something to teach them of the race that was overwhelmed with them. At Plymouth there is a rough rock, not unlike millions of others in New England, surrounded and guarded almost as if it was solid gold. It is the stone on which the feet of the Pilgrims first rested, as they landed on the forest covered shores of a new world, and from this spot, has gone forth, a marvelous influence greatly promoting the welfare of man, and which is destined to be far reaching and eternal.

This polished shaft, superbly mounted by a haughty but graceful female figure—a chaste and thoughtful tribute to the self-sacrificing devotion of woman in the great struggle—grasping an emblem of victory, although beautiful in design and faultless in execution, would be of little value were it not that it commemorates immortal deeds.

It requires heroic acts and a just cause, to make events that are fit for eternity. A brave deed in a righteous struggle, is as immortal as the soul of him who performs it. When Martin Luther, the great exponent of Christianity, three centuries ago, standing in the midst of the enslaved nations of Christendom, resisted the powers of the Papacy assembled in the Vatican, and defied the thunderbolts hurled at him from "that great city drunk with the blood of saints and martyrs," he communicated to the world a mighty impulse, and became the conspicuous leader in the greatest revolution ever effected in human affairs, and the work he did will live to the remotest hour of coming time. The brave and heroic deeds of old John Brown, done in the name of God and humanity, are marching on with his soul, and will still march on through the eternal ages. When Abraham Lincoln sent forth the edict " Let the bondman go free," a proclamation made possible and effective by the sublime heroism of the soldiers of the North, he not only thrilled the hearts of fettered millions, but he did a deed which will live, long after even the pyramids of Egypt shall have been sunk to the level of the Nile. A nobler cause than the defense of this mighty nation, when treason sought its overthrow, never aroused the patriotism, nor stirred to action, the heroism of humanity. Never in the conflict of human wills was there a mightier struggle, nor one freighted with vaster destinies, and never was a great demand more promptly and completely honored. It was the supreme moment in our national life. It was the hour when the patriotism of the American people was put to the vital test.

How did the sons of Nashua respond to this heroic and heaven born test? If this hour could be extended to a day, it would not be sufficient time, to give in detail the patriotic deeds of more than thirteen hundred of her noble soldiers who valiantly served the nation in its terrible ordeal of war. Among the many we recall the never to be forgotten William P. Ainsworth, young, energetic, brilliant, full of life and enthusiasm; he was among the first to go to the front. We remember his lithe figure, mounted on a superb horse, riding up and down these streets, recognized and loved by all. He fell at the head of his company, while charging the enemy, pierced with many bullets, one of the earliest and choicest offerings upon the altar of his country. John Q. A. Warren, (everybody's " Quin ") was shot through the heart at Georgia Landing, October 27, 1862, while shouting, " Come on boys, we'll lick 'em," displaying a bravery, as sublime as that of his great namesake at Bunker Hill. Edgerly, while in the Wilderness, and literally surrounded by rebels, swinging defiantly his sword, fell, pierced with a bayonet. Thompson and Hosley, Russell, Rogers, Button, Bennett, Davis, Towle, Tucker, Nottage, Danforth, Andrews, Sullivan, and scores of others who exhibited equal heroism, falling in the supreme hour, thus securing a fame that shall be deathless.

Among the noble dead, whose brave work now adorns its history, we also recall Timothy B. Crowley of the volunteer service, Lieutenant Thornton of the navy, and General John G.

THE ORATION.

Foster of the regular army. General Foster was one of the bravest and most distinguished officers of the Union forces in the great Civil War; educated at West Point, and having done splendid work in the Mexican War, he brought to the discharge of his great duties a perfect equipment, and his record is as bright and enduring as the stars. George Bowers, a born soldier, and a descendant of brave John Lovewell, was a gentleman and a patriot. The heroic deeds of his early career in the Mexican War, were fully equalled by his patriotic work in the Rebellion, and they stamp him as one of the most gallant and generous of Nashua's noble sons.

Aaron Fletcher Stevens, a leader in a great profession, in the full vigor of a splendid manhood, went to the front, did efficient work, received severe wounds from which he never recovered, and when peace once more triumphed, came home, and for years pursued again with marked success his life work, but at last, full of honors, passed on to his exceeding great reward; and when life's fitful fever was almost over, when delirium had taken captive the brain, the heart, true to its native loyalty, as the sunflower turns toward the sun, again yearned for the old flag; and as Napoleon, at St. Helena, in wild imagination, in his last hours, was once again at the head of the French army, so General Stevens, in his dying moments, was again at the head of his dear old regiment, and in the midst of a raging battle; and he triumphantly cried, "Steady, steady, we shall yet win the battle," and thus died, as true and noble a patriot, as ever drew breath.

Peace to the ashes, rest to the souls, and endless tributes to the memories of these laurel crowned patriots and their noble comrades. The work they performed in the great conflict deserves, and will receive, the everlasting homage of the city they so nobly honored, and the country they so gallantly and triumphantly served.

When the children of Israel had passed over Jordan, Joshua in obedience to the command of the Lord, set up twelve stones in the midst of Jordan, in the place where the feet of the priests which bore the ark of the covenant stood firm; and when they had been so placed, he said to the assembled multitude, "When your children shall ask their fathers in time to come, saying, 'What mean these stones?' then ye shall let your children know, Israel came over this Jordan on dry land, * * * and these stones shall be for a memorial unto the children of Israel forever. That all the people of the earth might know the hand of the Lord, that it is mighty." And so, when our children "shall ask their fathers in time to come, saying, 'what mean these stones?'" we shall say to them, that when red rebellion raised its ghastly hands, seizing this nation in its strangling grasp, and sought to destroy our government, perpetuate human slavery and drive freedom from this fair land, the feet of our noble sons, who bore aloft their country's flag, stood firm; and that all the world may know and forever remember their matchless fidelity. We shall say to them that these stones are for a memorial, intended "to save and recover from the deluge of time" the perpetual memory of deeds of such sublime patriotism, and of acts of such exalted worth, as to deserve eternal recognition by coming generations; that this shaft, whose very foundations were laid in sincere and humble gratitude for these sacrifices, is erected to constantly remind our countrymen, it may be through countless years, of a great civil war, in which were fought twenty-two hundred battles and skirmishes in four short years, and in which the havoc in affection, family ties, and all that makes life precious and worth living, is without a parallel in the history of the human race; and where the cost in cash and destruction of property no one could count in a life-time; and that in this mighty conflict, Nashua's gallant sons bravely fought, honoring by their splendid heroism, their homes, their city, their country, and their God.

This now consecrated shaft stands, not only as a grateful and expressive recognition of these unparalleled services, but it stands for more than this. It stands for the triumph of patriotism over treason, liberty over license, freedom over slavery, manhood over servitude, the school over the street, the home over the hovel, citizenship over the slave mart and the auction block, law over lawlessness, government over force and fraud and fetters. It stands an unwavering and eloquent witness, of the undying devotion of the fathers and mothers, the brave sons and the fair daughters of this great nation, on sea and on land, in peace and in war, to those sublime and eternal principles, which exalt the people and republics, and break down tyrants and empires. It stands, an impressive testimonial, to the triumph of that immortal prediction, made by the sainted Lincoln on the battle-stained field at Gettysburg, eighty-seven years after the birth of the nation, "That this nation, under God, shall have a new birth of freedom, and that the government of the people, by the people, for the people, shall not perish from the earth."

The American people have always been most fortunate in the character of the men who have fought their battles. It has been truly and quaintly said of the brave men who fought the early battles of New England, "they were not vagabonds and beggers and outcasts, of which armies are sometimes considerably made up, to run the hazard of war to avoid the dangers of starving; but they were the fathers and sons of the best of our families." This was conspicuously true of our Civil War. The best and noblest of the land engaged in the mighty conflict. They came from the farm, the shop, the store, the forge, the office, the counting room and school room, and from every profession and avocation. They were not idlers and loafers, but prosperous, energetic men, who had a vital interest in the welfare of the nation ; and they formed the most intelligent and invincible army that ever went forth in the defence of a country.

Montesquieu, a celebrated author, says : "In the birth of societies it is the chiefs of the Republic who form the institution, and in the sequel it is the institution which forms the chiefs of the Republic." In the formation of this Republic, it was the chiefs of our land who made its institutions, and now these institutions are making our chiefs. The United States were supremely blessed in the character of the people who first established their government. They were not only bold, energetic and conscientious, but they were broadly intelligent, They knew something of the experiences, the achievements and the failures of other nations, and they had the wisdom to be guided by their knowledge, and they established a government, which was not a conspiracy, but a noble compact, intended to secure universal benefit and freedom. The government in its turn has formed the national character of the people. Its citizens are unsurpassed in intelligence and earnest in their devotion, because they are the product of noble institutions ; they recognize the immense debt they owe their country ; they will peril their lives for it, because it deserves their affection and their heroism. The protection of a just government is the anchor of the human race. It is the infallible remedy, that destroys confusion and chaos, and establishes regularity and law. It protects home, property, and life : without it all the ambitions and aspirations and struggles of mankind, every human benefit, every virtue, every hope or expectation, every experience of love, every comfort or consolation, every grace or talent; all would be at the mercy of the mob.

There is no nation on earth which offers to its people such aids and inducements, such encouragement and protection as our own. When Burns, Scotland's great poet, sang the immortal song, "A man's a man for a' that," he voiced the principle upon which our government was intended to be established, and the great charm and value of the age and country in which we live is, that we can be just what we will, and that here every person, black or white, man or woman, has an equal chance in the race of life. Ours is not a government where a few hundred people hold the titles to all the landed estate of the nation. Here every person can own a home and an estate. This power to hold and own landed property, is a priceless right, and exerts a marvelous influence over the people of the United States. The stimulous of proprietorship is the most powerful that can be applied to labor. Stuart Mill says, "If there is a first principle in intellectual education it is this: that the discipline, which does good to the mind, is that in which it is active, not passive. The secret of developing the faculties is to give them much to do and much inducement to do it." Few things surpass in this respect, the occupation and ownership of property. A Swiss statistical writer speaks of the almost superhuman industry of peasant proprietors. Arthur Young says, "It is the magic of property that turns sand into gold." Michelet says, "It acts like a ruling passion in France." In Ireland, where the laborer does not own the soil he tills, there is a universal want of thrift, almost universal poverty and distress. Give a man the fee simple of the soil on which he works, and it blushes with untold charms, yields untold crops, and crowns him a nobleman.

CLOSING CEREMONIES.

A government which abounds in institutions so beneficent, in laws so just, in opportunities so magnificent; which protects the humblest as the most exalted; which disseminates intelligence and inculcates virtue among all its people; such a government cannot fail. A people, reared in such institutions, animated with the spirit of universal liberty, inspired with a sacred love of home and country, engaging in causes that are great and just, such a people cannot fail.

> "They never fail who die
> In a great cause; the block may soak their gore;
> Their heads may sodden in the sun; their limbs
> Be strung to city gates or castle walls;
> But still their spirit walks abroad. Though years
> Elapse, and others share as dark a doom,
> They but augment the deep and sweeping thoughts
> Which overspread all others, and conduct
> The world at last to freedom."

At the close of the oration by Mr. Burns, the military bands played some of the National airs.

His Honor, the Mayor then addressed the Commander of the Grand Army, saying.

Mr. Commander, our exercises are ended.

The ceremonies of the day were closed as follows:—

Commander.—Attention! comrades of the Grand Army of the Republic. As we close these services, the Guard of Honor is withdrawn, the symbols of the army and navy are removed, and the flag is lowered; but the memorial we have dedicated remains, guarded by the sacred memory of our dead. So long as it shall endure, it shall speak to us and to all future generations, of the patriotic fidelity and heroism displayed by our army and navy during the dark days of our country's history, and of that significant national authority, of which our flag is the symbol, to every brave, true and loyal American heart.

Officer of the Day, remove the symbols. Lower the flag. Dismiss the guard.

Chaplain. pronounce the benediction.

Chaplain.—The grace of our Lord and Saviour Jesus Christ, the love of God, and the communion of the Holy Spirit, be with us all. Amen.

Comrades.—Amen.

At the close of the ceremonies, which were ended as above, the Mayor briefly addressed the audience, and in the name of the City of Nashua, extended thanks to all who had honored the occasion with their presence, for their participation in the exercises of the day. The Mayor then declared the ceremonies ended, and ordered the Chief Marshal to dismiss the parade.

FINAL PROCEEDINGS.

FINAL PROCEEDINGS.

At the regular meeting of the City Government, held December 10, 1889, the following resolution was offered by His Honor, the Mayor, and passed unanimously :—

The City of Nashua, in token of her appreciation of the entire success that, in every stage, attended the building of the Soldiers' and Sailors' Monument.—erected the present year on Abbot Square, and dedicated on the 15th day of October last—and recognizing the hearty and unqualified approval which the object has received from her citizens; and observing with satisfaction that the public has set its seal of approval, not only on the structure itself, but also on the ceremonies attending the laying of the Corner-Stone and the Dedication, deems it proper to place on record an expression of her grateful acknowledgement to those who aided in the successful consummation of the undertaking; therefore,

Resolved, That, in addition to the thanks heretofore tendered to Col. Frank G. Noyes and Hon. Charles H. Burns, the orators, respectively, on the occasions of laying the Corner-Stone, and the Dedication,—the thanks of the City of Nashua, be hereby extended to—

The members of the Building Committee;

The members of the various committees, that arranged the plans and executed the details attending the Dedication;

The Grand Lodge of Free and Accepted Masons of the State of New Hampshire, George W. Currier, Grand Master;

The Grand Army of the Republic. Col. J. F. Grimes, Department Commander;

Mr. M. A. Taylor, Chief Marshal and his aids on the occasion of laying the Corner-Stone;

Col. E. J. Copp, Chief Marshal, and his aids on the occasion of the Dedication;

The guests and visitors, and to

All organizations and bodies, military and civic, which honored by their presence, the occasions of laying the Corner-Stone and Dedication of the Monument.

In Board of Mayor and Aldermen, December 10, 1889.

Passed.

CHARLES H. BURKE, Mayor.

In Board of Common Council, December 27, 1889.

Passed in concurrence.

HENRY P. WHITNEY, President.

NOTE.—The compiler of this volume—who has done his work at the request and under the supervision of the Building Committee,—desires to give credit to the Nashua Daily *Gazette*, and Nashua Daily *Telegraph* for the extracts he has made from those newspapers; to the Grand Master of Masons of New Hampshire; to the Commander of the Grand Army of the Republic for the Department of New Hampshire, and to the Chief Marshals on the days of the laying of the Corner-Stone, and Dedication of the Monument, for valuable information.

F. G. N.

Nashua, Dec. 1889.

www.ingramcontent.com/pod-product-compliance
Lightning Source LLC
Chambersburg PA
CBHW021917180426
43199CB00032B/432